Acceptance of European Social Sciences in Early Modern Asia

This work was supported by the National Research Foundation of Korea Grant funded by the Korean Government(NRF-2014S1A3A2037991)

Acceptance of European Social Sciences in Early Modern Asia

Edited by Dong-No Kim

YONSEI UNIVERSITY PRESS

Acceptance of European Social Sciences in Early Modern Asia

Edited by Dong-No Kim

Published in the Republic of Korea by Yonsei University Press,
Yonsei University, 50 Yonsei-ro Seodaemun-gu, Seoul, 03722, Republic of Korea
Tel : (82-2)2123-3380~2
Fax : (82-2)2123-8673
E-mail : ysup@yonsei.ac.kr
http://press.yonsei.ac.kr

Price ₩ 12,000
ISBN 978-89-6850-168-5 (93300)

CONTENTS

PREFACE

This book is the third publication in the research series created by the SSK 'Korean Social Sciences' Research Team of the Yonsei University Institute of State Governance Studies. The team has been conducting an empirical review of the genealogy of Korean social sciences in an attempt to explore its establishment and its developmental process. This joint study titled "The Intellectual Genealogy of Korean Social Sciences and A Plan to Develop Korean Theory of Social Sciences: From Acceptance to Development" launched in 2010. This study examines the way in which the social sciences became institutionalized as academic fields in Korea. I believe that it can cast light on the overall history and uniqueness of Korean social sciences.

The various academic fields of Korean social sciences were either developed according to autonomous standards or were institutionalized with the introduction of new concepts imported from abroad. Traditionally, the term "social science" was not widely used in Korea, although some ideologies of the Chosun dynasty were deeply rooted in the social sciences. With the dawning of the modern age and the inception of the crisis of the dynasty, these ideologies began to loose time-honored legitimacy and undergo a radical transformation. As they faced the difficulty in overcoming the crisis with the traditional literature, the Chosun intellectuals turned their attention outside their country, and realized that the secret of the West's wealth and power lay in modern knowledge. In this sense, we can say that the need for a new knowledge system was brought about by changes in the social environment.

This was also the case in the West. “Modern social sciences” emerged with the creation of modern societies and the subsequent need to study them. Although certain areas of the social sciences such as politics originated from ancient times, most of other fields were established as a form of modern academic disciplines to explain how modern societies emerged. As social conditions are intricately related to knowledge production, the research on the institutionalization of the Korean social sciences must also be explored from the historical viewpoint.

It was in this context that the SSK ‘Korean Social Sciences’ Research Team first examined the process by which the modern social sciences were introduced after the opening of the state and up to the colonial era. The research results were then compiled and published as a first research publication titled *Modern Conversion of Korean Society and the Acceptance of Western Social Sciences* (Seon In, 2013), along with a collection of raw materials. As a follow-up, we now publish a second and third collection of papers: the former in Korean and the latter in English. The second volume deals with the development of social sciences during the colonial period, while the third one covers both pre-colonial and colonial periods. Whereas the pre-colonial social sciences were mainly based on “translations” of the Western social sciences that were imported via Japan and were highly dependent on the efforts of individual scholars, the social sciences that were introduced during the colonial era originated from a greater variety of sources, and became institutionalized as an academic field.

This book examines how “social sciences” developed in the institutionalized modern education system of East Asia, especially Japan and Korea, paying special attention to some areas including politics, economics, and history. This book does not paint a complete picture of the East Asian acceptance of Western social sciences. However, I believe that this can give some understanding on the issue of the interaction of social sciences between Europe and East Asia in the process of the "introduction of modernity."

In this sense, I expect this book will provide an important insight into the way modern social sciences came to take root in Korea and Japan. I believe that the first step to evaluate the current state of our academic community is to look into our past. Therefore, this book is published in the hope that it will inspire many more scholars to take an interest in the issue and to produce more fruitful research results in the future.

Some chapters of this book have been published in academic journals: the earlier versions of the first chapter was published in *Ewah Sahak Yon'gu* and of the second chapter in *Asia Yon'gu*, the fourth chapter in *History of Economics Review*, and the last one in *Damron 201*. I want to deliver my gratitude to all these publishers and Taylor and Francis, which graciously permitted the reproduction of their papers. Last but not least, I am grateful to the National Research Foundation of Korea that provided the financial support for the publication of this book.

2016. 6.

Dong-No Kim

Director of the SSK 'Korean Social Sciences' Research Team

Institute of State Governance Studies at Yonsei University

CHAPTER 1.

Modernity and the Introduction of Western Social Science in Late Chosun*

Dong-No Kim**

Ⅰ. The Arrival of Western Modernity

The establishment of capitalism in the West and its subsequent union with imperialism opened a new period of global change. To invoke Immanuel Wallerstein's 'long 16th century' (1450-1640), a new world system would emerge, as the division of labor entwining Western and Eastern Europe expanded its reach beyond European borders. This early form of modern Western globalization would come to arrive at East Asia's doorsteps in the 19th century. The resulting encounters would lead to a veritable paradigm shift in the way that East Asia conceived its place in the world. It is in these contexts that we

---

* This paper is revised from the Korean version published in *Ewha Sahak Yon'gu* (『이화사학연구』), Volume 44, 2012.

** Professor, Department of Sociology, Yonsei University

examine the changes sweeping over Chosun dynasty Korea (henceforth, simply 'Chosun').

Encounters with foreign powers in the latter half of the 19th century led to a fundamental shift in the world views of those living in Chosun. The foreign powers now faced by Chosun were marked for their historically unprecedented scale—overwhelming not only Chosun, but also its neighbors, which had previously set the standards of foreign power (e.g. China and Japan). This external pressure, combined with centuries of internal corruption and political decay, triggered a national crisis within Chosun. In response, a number of proposals for overcoming these dire straits would come to the fore. Central amongst these was the debate on the need for Western culture and institutions in Chosun.

Of course, the 19th century did not entail Chosun's first encounter with the West. China had historically served as a gateway to the West. However, prior exposure to Western culture was both sporadic and limited. Further, while Chosun intellectuals and foreign officials were witness to Western incursions in China, it would take time before their experiences and the consequent proposal to adopt Western institutions would carry influence. Namely, it was not until the 1870s that the Enlightenment Party (*Kaewhapa*) would arise in the political sphere and attempt fundamental reforms in Chosun. Their influence would both advance the agenda for Western reforms and spur counter-proposals from Confucian scholars on how to reform the imploding Chosun state. The concurrent industrialization and modernization of the increasingly powerful Japanese Empire post-Meiji Restoration further stimulated this search for solutions.

Across various reform movements, the adoption of Western knowledge emerged as a top priority. The predominant view came to interpret

Western knowledge as the source of the West's wealth and power. Accordingly, attempts arose to introduce and institutionalize said knowledge. This view, which originated from the intellectual class, became prevalent as it propagated through newspapers and magazines. The establishment of new educational institutions was also particularly important in spreading this view across the general populace. The aim of this chapter is to investigate this very process through which Western knowledge—namely, Western social sciences—came to be introduced and adopted in late Chosun. Accordingly, this work posits and attempts to address the following questions: Why was Western knowledge perceived as necessary in late Chosun?; What were the social conditions mediating the adoption of Western knowledge?; and furthermore, how is it that the adoption of Western knowledge did not provoke larger conflicts with traditional forms of knowledge at the time?

These questions focus on the period between Chosun's forced opening with the Kwanghwa Treaty of 1876 and annexation by Japan in 1910. It relies on primary sources consisting of newspaper and magazine articles from the period. These sources provide insight on not only the ideas of the times, but also the impact of western ideas on Chosun. Consequently, this work aims to elucidate how intellectuals framed the challenge of introducing modernity into late Chosun, and how they premised the necessity of Western social sciences upon the challenges of their times.

II. The National Crisis and the Search for a Solution

While a number of motives can be identified underlying the call to adopt Western institutions, one stands out above the rest: the need to overcome national crisis. This national crisis can be characterized as a total or all-encompassing one.[1] Externally, the fall of neighboring China—the former center of the world—under Western invasion heralded similar prospects for Chosun. This was further compounded by an internal situation characterized by centuries of corruption and political decay. Dire circumstances initiated a search for a means to overcome this crisis, which in turn produced early forms of Chosun modernity. While some advocated independent forms of modernization, late Chosun modernizers, on the whole, viewed Western institutions as an essential ingredient for realizing modernity.

What, then, were these Western institutions sought by late Chosun modernizers? Generally, modernity in the West is often characterized by the rise of nation-states, development of a capitalist economy, nationalistic forms of social cohesion, and a shift from collectivist to individualist modes (Giddens, 1990). Modernity in Chosun, at first glance, shared similar characteristics. Reforms aimed for a modern state based on constitutional law, economic development through the promotion of industry, the establishment of individualistic human rights, and unification through nationalism. However, closer scrutiny of such reforms also reveals some differences. Attempts to overcome crisis in Chosun focused on the establishment of a modern state and the development of the economy via promotion of industry and commerce. Here, we consider why Western social science was viewed as necessary in order to achieve these goals, and in what particular form.

A variety of opinions can be observed amongst Chosun intellectuals

---

[1] For more on the characteristics of this all-encompassing crisis, see Kim (2009: Chapter 1).

and political elites in regards to the type of Western institutions required for Chosun reforms. For example, mild reformers, also known as 'Western technology, Eastern ways (東道西器論)' theorists, advocated minimal imports from the West, stressing the need to localize foreign technology. On the other hand, radical reformers, or 'legal reform (變法論)' theorists, advocated the wholesale transplantation of Western institutions. Going even further, some revolutionaries, or 'enlightened civilization (文明開化論)' theorists, even viewed the adoption of Western religion as necessary for Chosun modernization.[2]

Broader attitudes towards the West were similarly diverse. However, with the exception of some Confucian scholars advocating 'reject heterodoxy, keep orthodoxy (斥邪衛正論)' theorists, most saw the introduction of some form of Western institutions as unavoidable. It is in these contexts that arguments can be found on the necessity of Western scholarship. Namely, the strength of Western empire was attributed to their superior knowledge. Consequently, adopting this knowledge would provide a means for Chosun to overcome its national crisis. This argument can be found in many publications from the period, such as the following article from the *Dokrib Shinmun* (*The Independent*) from 1898:

> There are reasons for the wealth and power of the West and for the poverty and weakness of Korea. Western nations, through their respect for practical knowledge, invented new technology and became the first to advance across the world. Western nations respect practical knowledge, invent new civilized tools, got stronger than ever, and became the first to advance in the world.

---

2 For more on the contrasting positions regarding the introduction of Western institutions, see Kim (2004a); Kim (2004b)

> On the contrary, Korea only respects empty knowledge, and cannot face the Western nations.[3]

Thus, the difference in wealth and power between Chosun and the West was recognized as stemming from a difference in knowledge. In other words, the secret to superior Western civilization and technology lay in the practical knowledge of the West. This stance was not exclusive to *Dokrib Shinmun*, which was affiliated with the Enlightenment Party. It can also be found in the writings of Confucian reformists. For example, an article in *Gihoheunghakhoe Wolbo* (畿湖興學會月報) by Young-jin Yoon (1908a) states that "Westerners view the knowledge of the people as source of the perseverance of one's country. Enlightened progress of a country and the civilization of humankind depends partly on the free energies of society and partly on the competitive spirit between ethnic races." Thus, this argument that knowledge determines the fate of a nation also implicates Western knowledge as the source of Western superiority.

Interest in Japan, which arose as a new power in East Asia alongside the West, unfolded in a similar manner. An article in *Dokrib Shinmun* points to "the education of the people and enforcement of just laws" as source of Japan's newfound wealth and power.[4] Furthermore, Japan followed Western experience in order to realize these elements. It is in this dimension that The Independence strongly argued for the need to translate and widely disseminate Western knowledge. Another article published earlier that year, for example, states that there exists no other

---

[3] *Dokrib Shinmun* (June 14, 1898).

[4] *Dokrib Shinmun* (December 3, 1896).

undertaking more pressing or more profitable for Chosun than the translation, publication, and dissemination of Western texts.[5]

These arguments started arising in the 1880s, such as with the Chosun official Yun-Joong Oe (魚允中), who proposed the establishment of schools that adopted Western knowledge. Another example is a royal edict from 22 June 1894, which elucidates plans for a modern educational system during the Kabo Reform (Wang, 2003: 304). While the Kabo Reform failed to realize such plans, interest in Western knowledge continued to increase amidst the search for a practical means to rescue Chosun from sovereign crisis. Accordingly, it was Western social science, which directly touched upon the situation faced by Chosun, that attracted the most attention. An 1899 article from Dokrib Shinmun, for example, states that "as one cannot be influential in politics without studying sociology, state science, public administration, vocational science, finance, philosophy, it is necessary to teach this knowledge to the youth so that they can become the force behind the rise of this nation."[6] Here, we can identify the Western scholarly fields viewed as most necessary for Chosun contexts.[7] Endowing Chosun political actors with such knowledge would consequently enable a wealthy and powerful Chosun.

Similar views can also be found in *The Hwangseong Shinmun* (皇城新聞), which was led by Confucian reformists. The argument here lay in advancing Western knowledge (e.g. law, world geography, world history) in tandem with incumbent knowledge (e.g. Chosun geography, Chosun

---

5 *Dokrib Shinmun* (June 2, 1896).

6 *Dokrib Shinmun* (January 14, 1899).

7 Many arguments arose in those times in regards to the many fields of social science to be introduced. Intellectuals of the times expressed great interested in politics, economics, and law, while showing relatively limited interest in military science.

history). In contrast to the *Dokrib Shinmun*, frontispiece of Enlightenment Party reformers, the views of *The Hwangseong Shinmun* can be seen as an attempt to introduce Western knowledge while holding on to Confucian foundations. Both parties, however, share in their fundamental motives and means; that is, of overcoming state crisis by utilizing Western knowledge. It is in this respect that a widespread social consensus can be identified in the critical need to introduce Western social sciences, such as politics, economics, and law. These studies were seen as providing the necessary knowledge not only for domestic institutional reform, but also for overcoming the catastrophe of a potential loss of sovereignty.[8]

III. The National Crisis and the Introduction of Western Knowledge

1. The establishment of a new political system and the introduction of political science

Amidst the various attempts to overcome crisis in Chosun, the highest priority was to establish a new political system. After the Kabo Reformers' attempt at rapid modernization, the question of what kind of political system to pursue became the subject of endless debate. The Kabo Reform attempted an extensive transformation towards a modern state by weakening royal authority and centralizing power in the government cabinet (Kim, 2009: Ch. 4). The cabinet replaced the traditional six ministry system (六曹) and the State Council (議政府) with eight ministries in

[8] While some works from this period also make reference to moral philosophy and the humanities, such fields were imbued with relatively less importance.

a constitutional government. The Kabo Reform, however, ended in failure, and the debate on political systems—particularly monarchy versus constitutional governance—continued on into the subsequent establishment of the Great Korean Empire.

On one side, Kojong and his conservative bureaucrats sought to restore the monarchy and strengthen the royal authority of the emperor. On the other, enlightened civilization theorists sought a constitutional state. Amidst this conflict stood the questions of how to build a proper modern state and on how to locate oneself within it. In these regards, traditional Confucianism had plenty of knowledge to offer. However, the discourse came to focus instead on Western political science, amidst larger currents that emphasized the construction of a Western modern state system. Consequently, many Western political concepts and theories came to be translated and introduced to late Chosun society in attempt to bolster the foundations of new state-building efforts.

A central argument that came to be presented here is that Western political science was necessary to transform a backwards country like Chosun into an advanced one. An article in the *Daehanheunghakbo* (大韓興學報) from 1909 argues that "as Japan is learning Western political science and China is learning Japanese political science, it is the duty of the backwards nation to research and profit from the political science of advanced nations (*Daehanheunghakbo*, 1909)." Little doubt was thus expressed in regards to the necessity of introducing Western political science for the sake of Chosun development. The most fundamental problem in this attempt was how to define a state. The following excerpt by Gi Lee(李沂) in a 1908 issue of the *Honamhakbo* (湖南學報) is particularly revealing:

> Three tasks are necessary for building the community of citizens, or the state. First is land... Second is the people. The many subjects must be brought together, or there is no use to their number, however large, if they cannot be in contact. Third is sovereignty...[9]

The above text defines the state as a community constituted by land, citizens, and sovereign authority. If one changes a few of the terms to their 'modern' equivalents (e.g. from land '토지' to territory '영토', or subjects '신민' to national citizens '국민'), the resulting explanation is remarkably similar to those found in present-day introductory political science textbooks. This particular passage can be seen as revealing the early spread of the concept of the modern Western state. What is peculiar here, however, is its approach on defining the state from not an individualistic stance, but rather a collectivist one. This can be understood in the contexts of the present crisis, which called for collectivist over individualistic efforts. As will be seen, this tendency manifests in many more publications of the times.

A new conception of the citizen—the fundamental unit constituting the state—was also laid out. Completely different than before, it was now the free individual that was the main political agent. In particular, many diverse ideas on civil liberties, based upon natural rights theory, were argued by the Independence Club (Dokrib Hyobhoe) (Shin, 1975: Ch. 3). As the notion of the rights of a free and equal individual came to the fore, so too did a variety of Western political theories that served as the premises.[10] Here, however, it is necessary to be mindful of whether

---

[9] Lee (1908a).

[10] For example, Rousseau's 'social contract' was translated and published as 'minyakron'

the free individual of some enlightened civilization thinkers from the Independence Club were identical to the Western individual that was completely separate from the traditional community. Rather, it may be more accurate to view Chosun individualism as squarely tied to collectivist contexts, in a seemingly paradoxical sort of communal individualism (Kim, 1999: 53). It is also worthwhile to note that the community indicated by these progressive Chosun thinkers was not that of the traditional family and village, but rather that of the new modern state (i.e. the national community). In this respect, the individual, as a political agent, was endowed with a new identity; that of the 'national citizen'. This would further need a new sort of consciousness.

This need was reflected in the vigorous political debates that unfolded in regards to the concept, rights, and duties of a 'national citizen'. For example, Dong-Sook Cho (趙東肅) wrote in 1908 that "on the whole, nation-states have a form and a spirit. The people constituting this form and spirit are its citizens. Thus, as national progress depend on the progress of its peoples' abilities, national strength is gathered from individual strengths and national wisdom is gathered from individual wisdoms (Cho, 1908)." Jo thus emphasized the importance of the people's task in the formation and operation of a nation. The key factor behind national progress is the progress of the individuals constituting the state. At the same time, national strength can be said to be strengthened through the unification of individuals. Accordingly, the question of how to mold the new national citizen became the central challenge behind achieving political modernization and overcoming national crisis.

The need for citizens holding this new national identity is expressed

---

(民約論). See Kim (2000: 651).

in a number of works—particularly in *Daehanmaeil Shinbo* (大韓每日申報).[11] A number of its serials even go so far as to introduce the virtues of the new citizen, which included the following: pursuit of public over private interests, prioritization of duties in regards to rights, and fostering a love of one's country.[12] This national identity stands in marked contrast to the identity of traditional subjects and even, to some extent, with ethnic identity. For example, one article states that "national citizens have a shared ancestry, history, religion, language, mind, and intellect that produces unified internal action, as if they constitute the bones and muscles of a single body. This spirit, which does not rely on one reason, is the national citizen."[13] This elucidates the distinction between national and ethnic identity. As seen in this excerpt, national citizens that constitute the new state go beyond shared territory or cultural heritage to share a conscious identity, which further enables political actors to act together for the sake of the nation. One can quite possibly perceive similarities with the collective identity found in forms of the modern Western state.

It was thus posited that failure in creating a national identity that wedded the individual with the state would lead to crisis. Conversely, if citizens accepted their new identities and faithfully carried out their duties, then the state would become wealthy and powerful.[14] Accordingly,

---

11 *Daehanmaeil Shinbo* (February 1910; February 23, 1910).

12 *Daehanmaeil Shinbo* (October 18, 1905; November 20, 1906).

13 *Daehanmaeil Shinbo* (July 30, 1908). *Daehanmaeil Shinbo* (February 22, 1910) also connected the identity of the new national citizen with national wealth and power in stating that "If Korea is to find its way out of crisis and enjoy happiness and comfort, it must reach the grounds of wealth and power, shine light upon the present international dangers, and, further, shape its present compatriots into 20th century national citizens."

14 Ik-Yong Kim (1908) writes that "as good results can only be acquired through the

it was necessary to raise the new modern state upon the foundations of a patriotic national citizenry. This would strengthen the nation's sovereignty, and it was towards these ends that the advancement of people's rights was viewed as not mutually exclusive, but rather complementary and necessary for securing national sovereignty.

As such conceptions of the new modern state and its citizens—both fundamental notions in Western political science—were introduced, so too were many other new concepts and foreign political systems. In particular, Aristotle's classification of political systems (e.g. monarchy, republic, aristocracy, democracy) attempted in Politics widened the scope of understanding and introduced the principle of separation of power (i.e. legal, administrative, judicial) as a means for defending against autocratic politics.[15]

Vigorous debates on the future political system unfolded alongside the introduction of these diverse political theories. It is important to remember here that Chosun intellectuals accepted Western political science for the practical purposes of addressing political realities and not for purely theoretical ends. That is, Western political science was introduced as a means of overcoming national crisis, and its theories became necessary education for political elites. The following excerpt from *Dokrib Shinmun* provides a clear example:

> The study of politics is a discipline from enlightened nations that arose over millennia and through the efforts of tens of thousands of thinkers. It is im-

---

fulfillment the citizens' duty, the dereliction of negligence of such duty causes not just a big problem, but also poses a real danger to the nation."

15 *Daehanmaeil Shinbo* (November 1, 1905); Ahn (1908); Pubyul Dokseoin (法律讀書人) (1908).

> proper to be a government official without learning these studies... If politics is not taught, then there will be no appropriate persons to entrust with the responsibilities of governing.[16]

In this way, the teaching and use of Western political science became an important subject in the contexts of a Chosun state facing national crisis.

2. The introduction of constitutional governance and the discipline of law

Efforts to establish a new modern state entailed the consequent challenge of determining the appropriate structure and form of governance. After the Kwangmu Reform, which followed the Kabo Reform, fierce debate unfolded between Confucian reformists, progressive cultural enlightenment thinkers, and Kojong and his conservative bureaucrats in regards to who should reign and in what manner. Amidst the many aspects of modernity introduced after the Kabo Reform, one that stood out was the establishment of the rule of law. Transforming the monarchy into a modern form of governance, which was ruled by law, can be viewed as the essence of the Kabo Reform. It can be further viewed as an attempt to establish a form of government following Max Weber's rational-legal authority (Weber, 1978: 217-223). Within three very active months following the establishment of a new government in June 1894, a huge volume of legislation (around 200 bills) was passed. While this productivity was made possible, in part, due to the active referencing of

---

[16] *Daehanmaeil Shinbo* (April 14, 1894).

prior laws (e.g. Taejeonhoetong, 大典會通), these new regulations also made use of new foreign bodies of law ('corpus juris'), such as Japan's (Wang, 2003: 211).

This trend largely carried through into the Kwangmu Reform under Kojong and his conservative bureaucrats. In July 1899, Kojong ordered the establishment of the Regulatory Review Bureau (法規校正所) and declared a royal edict demanding "the election of individuals well acquainted with law and with expert reasoning to produce proper regulations (Sung, 2003: 112-113)." While the process of making and implementing new laws was anything but smooth and came to face many conflicts, legal legislation and the demand for the rule of law became established as irreversible currents.

The demand for the rule of law, much like with the establishment of a new modern state, was intimately tied to the search for a way out of national crisis. As such, it also reflected practical political realities versus pure theoretical interests. The most fundamental subject amongst discussions on the rule of law was that of constitutional governance. After a system of governance that severely curbed royal authority was planned during the Kabo Reform, the question of where to position the monarchy became a central issue for the state reform movement. After the establishment of the Kwangmu government, Kojong viewed autocracy as a possible means for laying the foundations for independence in the face of foreign invasion (Lee, 2000: 78). However, as most political elites did not consider autocracy as a viable means for increasing individual liberties. As such, autocracy did not provide a feasible path towards national wealth and power, and they instead identified with the need for a constitution. As most Western states took the form of constitutional governments, this was also viewed as an origin of superior Western power. The following excerpt written by Hyo-Jung Yoon (尹孝定) provides an apt description from the times:

> The spirit of a constitutional government lies in the monarchy and the people. Here, state affairs must be decided upon through consensus between top and bottom, and the prior operational foundations are based upon the chosen political parties and public assemblies of the people. The characteristic traits of an autocracy are unlimited royal authority, weak civil liberties, and division between top and bottom. Here, prior institutions operate through the threat of absolute tyranny, and are subject to aristocrats who enshrine the monarchy. Comparing and deducing the pros and cons of these two present political systems is up to the patriotic citizen.[17]

Underlying this passage is the notion that the center of constitutional governance was the unification of royalty and the people to make the patriotic individual the key political agent. The reasoning here is that constitutional governments were able to develop by enhancing the patriotism of its citizens and, thus, its social unification.

In this respect, the highest priority amongst those interested in legal studies was constitutional law. *Daehanmaeil Shinbo* connects constitutional law with political systems as follows: "As a constitution codifies all of a state's laws, all governments—whether autocratic, constitutional, or republican—fall under constitutionalism."[18] *Jekuk Shinmun* also carried many pieces on constitutional law, including introductions on the constitutional law systems of various countries around the world. Furthermore,

---

17 Yoon (1906).

18 *Daehanmaeil Shinbo* (October 18, 1905).

Sung-Gu Cho (趙聲九) published a text entitled Constitutional Law (憲法) in 1907, followed by three more texts the following year with the same title, written by Chi-Hyung Yoo (兪致衡), Sang-Yun Kim (金祥演), and Seung-Bin Park (朴勝彬), respectively. Finally, the publication of translated versions of Japanese scholarly works on constitutional law adds yet another indication of the interest in constitutional law at the time (Kim, 2000: 105, 168-169, 745-752).

The theories from constitutional law and broader legal studies were also widely introduced. *Dokrib Shinmun*, for example, offers that "the most urgent task—one which citizens cannot afford to forget for even a moment—is first, knowledge, and second, law."[19] Furthermore, "law guides the people to watch their words and behave properly with respect to social morals and customs, similar to one's personal food and dress." It was to this extent that law was considered to be essential for those living in a modern state. As traditional Chosun regulations were unfortunately inconsistent with the newly forming modern society, discussions on law at the time generally focused on foreign laws introduced from the West. Bo-sang Kwon (權輔相), for example, argues the inescapability of Western law, writing that "the so-called constitutional law, civil law, commercial law, contract law of present civilized empires are Western and thus untraditional. It is necessary to reform Eastern legal thought in order to acquire these new examples from West (Kwon, 1908)." As such, new foundations for the rule of law were laid with the introduction of diverse fields of Western law. These included contract law, property law, corporate law, and bankruptcy law—many of which directly related to the political domain.

[19] *Dokrib Shinmun* (April 12, 1899).

The introduction of Western law under the contexts of overcoming national crisis carried inherent political motives. At home, this entailed the protection and control of citizens. Abroad, this entailed the protection of Chosun sovereignty in a foreign world system. For example, newspaper and magazine articles published at the time emphasized the protection of individuals to be gained under the rule of law. For example, an 1899 excerpt from *Dokrib Shinmun* explains that "we need to rely on laws in order protect the lives and property of the people and to secure the foundations of the country."[20] Additionally, an article from *Daehanmaeil Shinbo* includes that "generally, as the laws of well governed nations protect the people, there is a need to research these laws. On the other hand, poorly governed countries have laws that restrict and ruin the people."[21] In this manner, the article directly connects protection of the individual with government by law. Following this stance, the protection or suppression of the individual citizen under the rule of law ultimately produced a well- or poorly-governed nation. Similarly, this too could determine the capabilities of the Chosun state.

Another important factor in the introduction of Western law is the notion that the rule of law could legitimize the control of individuals and maintain social order. For example, an article in *Daedonghakhoe Wolbo* (大東學會月報) writes that "the state needs regulations that set limits to individual behavior in order to prevent violent and disruptive behavior. Confusion must be dismantled and eliminated in order to maintain social order and, at the same time, manage full individual lives. Law is a root cause enabling such state governance over great numbers

20 *Dokrib Shinmun* (March 3, 1899).

21 *Daehanmaeil Shinbo* (November 11, 1908).

of humankind (Doo, 2008)." This article, which finds a root motive behind the emergence of law in the control of individuals, presents such control as beneficial for the maintenance of social order and the realizing of full individual lives. In order words, law enabled a consensus between state and individual interests by fulfilling the state's original purpose of maintaining social order, in tandem with the safety and happiness of individuals.

Another important political motive driving the introduction of academic Western law was the intent to protect Chosun sovereignty by understanding international law. After the pain of ignorance experience by Chosun during its forced opening through the Kwanghwa Treaty of 1876, the necessity of understanding international law was elevated to new heights. As texts such as *Mankuk Kongpub* (Elements of International Law or 萬國公法), *Chosun Cheakryak* (Chosun Strategy or 朝鮮策略), *Yion* (易言), and *Kongpub Hoetong* (International Law of Civilized States or 公法會通) spread their influence in Chosun society, Chosun sought a way to protect its autonomy amidst world powers through the analysis of international law.[22] As translated works from Western international law scholars and from Chinese scholars influenced by Western international law were introduced into Chosun, arguments arose for new diplo-

22 As is widely known, *Chosun Chaekryak* describes the foreign policy strategies of Chosun, Japan, and China in facing Russia, as documented by Chinese scholar-official Zunxian Huang (黃遵憲). *Yion*(塵檲) was also written by a Chinese national, Guanying Zheng (鄭觀應), and espouses the introduction of international law as a means to reduce international conflict and to promote reconciliation. *Mankuk Kongpub* (萬國公法) was written by US scholar Henry Wheaton and translated by missionary William Martin. Martin also translated *Kongpub Hoetong* (公法會通), which was written by Johann Bluntschli (German title: '*Das moderne Völkerrecht der civilisirten Staten*'). For more relating to these, see Kim (2000) and Oh (2004).

matic strategies based upon international influence and equal diplomacy to secure autonomy.

Amidst the incursions of foreign powers and a national crisis, international laws' balance-of-power theory, which held that small and weak countries could preserve their sovereignty by balancing the influence of world powers, seemed to spell salvation to Chosun intellectuals (Oh, 2004: 128). Of course, the fact that international politics followed not the principles of international law but the realities of self-interest soon came to the fore under the critiques of reformist Confucians such as Eun-Sik Park and Che-Ho Shin (Kim, 1994: 403). Despite this, however, continued expectations regarding international law led to critiques on the outcomes of the Japan-Korea Protectorate Treaty from the perspective of international law and exasperated sighs in the assertions that Chosun did not know how to ally with foreign countries because it did not understand law and treaties.[23]

3. Modern economic development and the introduction of economics

Economic development through the promotion of industry and commerce accompanied modern state reform as another important path towards overcoming national crisis. After the attempt to introduce a modern currency-based economy under the Kabo Reform's cash payment tax system, various plans were discussed on how to spur economic development through the promotion of industry and commerce. Diverse aspects of the modern economy were introduced, such as the unification of weights and measures, the modification of the currency system, and the im-

---

23 *Daehanmaeil Shinbo* (November 1, 1906; July 23, 1910).

plementation of related economic infrastructure. Even after the enlightenment theorists who led the Kabo Reform fell out of power, their representative paper, *Dokrib Shinmun*, continued to emphasize the importance of promoting industry. In this stance, the views of the Confucian reformists did not much differ (Kim, 1999: 140-147; Kim, 2009).

Throughout the transition of power from Kabo Reformers to Kojong's conservative bureaucrats, there emerged significant attempts to realize modern economic development. Kojong's Kwangmu Reform emphasized the promotion of industry and commerce as an important issue, with past and present bureaucrats even turning to business as emphasis was placed on the establishment of new companies (Kang, 1973: 17). The royal family was particularly active in leading this modernization effort. For example, Yong-Ik Lee, who managed the royal assets, also led the administration of mines, the direction of railway operations, the implementation of a modern currency system, and the establishment of the central bank (Suh, 2003: 118-119). Various fundamental institutions were established to enable capitalist economic development, and private banks began to emerge under government backing, such as Daehan Chunil Bank (大韓天一銀行). A prominent characteristic of this period is the broad extent of state involvement in leading economic modernization.

Attempts to introduce modern Western economics arose in conjunction with these above trends. First and foremost, it was necessary to introduce the definition and meaning of economics. Here, Sung-Hee Yoon (尹成熙) states in 1908 that "the human temperament is naturally not good at being many things at once. Thick or thin, diligent or lazy, spendthrift of wasteful—such temperaments must be taught in order to properly research the relationship between things. This is what economics does (Yoon, 1908b)." In other words, because humans possess different individual traits, it is necessary to artificially adjust individuals in order to form proper relations. Studying economic principles provides just such knowledge.

Many economic terms were also introduced alongside definitions of economics. Basic concepts in economics (e.g. commodities, free goods, desires, value, production, distribution, exchange, consumption) were introduced and defined in various ways.[24] Meanwhile, Japanese scholars who had studied abroad actively tried to introduce Western economic theory through various magazines, and even spurred interest in foreign entrepreneurs.[25] An article in *Daedonghakhoe Wolbo* introduces the diverse variety of companies (e.g. joint-stock company, corporation, joint-stock limited partnership) and their importance in the development of industry and commerce.[26]

Underlying these diverse ways in which economics was introduced was the pragmatic aim of utilizing such knowledge to increase the nation's wealth. Again, national crisis demanded a means to strengthen the nation—in this case, via economic development. In this dimension, an editorial published in *Daehanmaeil Shinbo* (April 8, 1909) writes, "Compatriots, if we cannot correct the dangers causing economic panic, in the end, men and women both old and young will be out on the streets. The present system is lost in old knowledge and collapsing. Compatriots, we must find and implement rules to quickly fix this." In

---

24 See, for example, Yoon (1907); Moon (1908a); and Lee (1908b).

25 Such attempts can be seen across articles in the *Gongsuhakbo* (共修學報), *Rakdongchinmokhoe Hakbo* (洛東親睦會學報), and Sanghakgye (商學界). The *Daehanmaeil Shinbo* (大韓每日申報) also carries frequent articles on foreign entrepreneurs (e.g. *Daehanmaeil Shinbo*, September 7, 1907).

26 Pubyul Dokseoin (法律讀書人) (1909).

this writing, a thesis is put forth that the failure to identify the causes of economic crisis and implement appropriate measures will soon lead to the fall of the nation. Further, it emphasizes the importance of the economy in determining the fate of the nation.

Following this logic, the economic development achieved by individuals is not localized to the individual dimension, but rather connected to the welfare of the state. Another article in *Daehanmaeil Shinbo* (October 31, 1905) states that "if commerce is weak and commercial power cannot be advanced, then national sovereignty will also crash." This kind of stance ultimately implies utilitarian logic equating national wealth with aggregate individual wealth. In this aspect, theories on the creation of national wealth from individual economic behavior from Adam Smith occupied an important role even in Chosun, as evidenced in published articles introducing Smith's theories (Moon, 1908b).

Moving beyond this stance on individual and national wealth, contributing factors to economic development also included the fulfillment of national duty by the citizens. The following passage provides an exemplary expression of this stance:

> One needs to set one's own upright way of living if one is to uphold the status of one's society. If one wishes to fulfill the duties of a national citizen, it will not be possible to do so without knowledge of socio-economic phenomena. Without learning economic thought under specialists, not only will one fail in one's individual goals, society will also fail in its own goals. For these reasons, one needs to learn economics.[27]

---

[27] Han (1909).

In this excerpt, knowledge of economics is presented as a basic virtue necessary for individuals living in a national community, and reveals economic development as a necessary element for bolstering national strength.

A noteworthy aspect of this discourse is the perceived necessity of protecting individuals under the rule of law in order to realize economic development. The aforementioned protection of individuals under the rule of law entailed both individual civil liberties and property rights. For example, Wan-young Ryu (柳完永) writes in 1907 that "If the economy is satisfactory but there is no law, then there is nothing protecting the economy... A society where the strong eat the weak will not be able to produce strong national foundations (Ryu, 1907)." In other words, if economic activity lacks legal protection, the uncertainty of its results deteriorates the foundations of the state. This exhibits similarities with social contract theory, such as that of Hobbes and Locke, who found basis for the existence of the state in the establishment of laws to protect economic interests.

It was stressed that the establishment of a fair legal system ensures stable economic activity and can also raise the trustworthiness of economic transactions (*Hwangseong Sinmun*, April 5, 1899). This can also be related to social capital theory on the establishment of trust relationships and reduction of transaction costs found in contemporary sociology. Accordingly, the introduction and application of modern law in the economic domain can be seen as having made a significant contribution in laying the social foundations for modern capitalist economic development.

IV. Concluding Remarks: Harmonizing Modernity with Tradition

To the extent that the introduction of modernity in Korea came from without, we need to think about its relationship with traditional society. The relationship between the two is mediated by the national crisis that necessitated the introduction of foreign cultural institutions to the traditional Korean society. While there might be differences in the degree to which this crisis determined the import of foreign cultural institutions, it is clear that such contexts would have made it very difficult to reject Western knowledge. It is also due to this crisis that the practical content of Western social science (particularly in politics, law, and economics) was prioritized over the humanities and other Western scholarship. Further, priority was also placed on practical substance over pure theory when importing Western social science.

It was also because of this national crisis that the introduction of Western social science produced relatively few conflicts with comparative traditional elements. Broadly speaking, the introduction of foreign matter always carries the possibility of conflicting with incumbent traditions. Accordingly, these conflicts present an important aspect for understanding the introduction of Western knowledge. Here, an explanation of the relative absence of conflict in the Chosun case relies on the conditions of national crisis and other factors of the time.

Of course, some attitudes wholeheartedly rejecting Western knowledge did arise. At times, some would attempt to unilaterally reject Western knowledge. At others, the same attempt would be made but in reverse, attacking traditional knowledge. For example, *Dokrib Shinmun* strongly critiques traditional Confucian scholars who attempt to satisfy themselves with the words of the old sages, stating that "Eastern knowledge is like a person inside a tall wall, while Western knowledge is like a person on top of a tall mountain." Accordingly, even if it took effort, "the higher one goes, the more scenes of the plants, trees, mountains, and streams. One needs to study in order to enjoy such higher learning (*Dokrib Shinmun*, June 14, 1898)."

This kind of combative stance, which also evidence the emergence of the enlightened civilization theorists, began to appear every now and then. More frequently observed, however, are the unfolding efforts to harmonize Western and traditional Chosun knowledge. In this respect, it is worth pointing out the following stance from Confucian reformists in their representative paper, *Daehanmaeil Shinbo*:

> There are presently two problems faced in learning and thought. One is that, because our country's thought is deep, we do not enjoy foreign scholarship. The other is that, because we become infatuated with foreign scholarship, our country's thought disappears. If many decades of effort are not put into syncretizing our thought with foreign scholarship, it will not be easy to expand said thought and scholarship.[28]

In the end, the question of how to harmonize exogenous modernity and endogenous tradition becomes the key cause leading to reduced conflicts with Western knowledge. Many intellectuals of the time attempted to resolve this issue by interpreting foreign Western knowledge from a traditional Confucian point of view. To do this, new interpretations of Confucianism were first needed. For example, Confucian reformists began to assert that some conservative Confucians did not properly under-

[28] *Daehanmaeil Shinbo [Korean Daily News]* (16 July 1910).

stand the original (or genuine) meaning of accommodation (隋時變通) (Kim, 1994: 54). Similarly, Eun-sik Park (朴殷植) argues that Western learning needs to be introduced in order to carry out new education for all citizens, proposing "Western knowledge and new knowledge education at the center. Do not throw away the Confucian education of Confucius and Mencius, but rather reform it to keep the parts that are appropriate (Shin, 2010: 514-515)."

Such attempts to utilize Western learning as a foundation for Confucianism was common. For example, there were attempts to lay foundations of combined rule by the royalty and the people to increase individual civil liberties, and Western natural rights theory was even used to reflect upon Confucian theory on human nature. Natural rights, which was translated as "chun-bu' (天賦, or roughly, 'endowments from the heavens'), was understood in the first passage of *Joong-yong* (中庸) in terms of the mandate from heaven (天命). This was, in turn, accepted as the natural reasons of a moral and gendered human nature (Chung, 2004: 171-172).

Similar circumstances can also be found in the understanding of international law. A translation of an important text on international law, International Law (萬國公法), understood its central idea—the balance of power—as a basis for natural law theory. Most critically, natural law theory was interpreted here again through Confucian concepts and reasoning. Sample excerpts include "educated countries possess benevolence and righteousness" and "because public law stands upon the foundations of human character, it is appropriate for humankind and stands in line with state law." Here, the Korean texts utilize Confucian conceptions such as natural law (天理), benevolence and righteousness (仁義), and human character (人性), which would have significantly contributed to ease of understanding for Chosun intellectuals (Oh, 2004: 127-128).

As the above examples demonstrate, Western knowledge was apt for interpretation through a Confucian perspective. Consequently, potential conflicts between traditional and modern knowledge were reduced, and foreign knowledge was able to sprout new roots in Chosun. The fact that Western knowledge crossed through China and Japan may also be an important factor contributing to this phenomenon. As in the International Law text, Korean versions of Western texts translated in China contained significant portions that could be compatible with Confucian thought. This is likely to have correlations with the reforms of Chinese intellectuals and their proposed form of modernity, which quickly abandoned traditional Confucianism but still held on to an inherent Confucian identity (Grieder, 1981: 131).[29] In this sense, the 'double translations (or second-hand translation)' of Western texts into Chinese and then Korean may have enabled more uniform and easily understood translations than through direct translations, alone.

[29] A representative figure with this attitude is Youwei Jiang (姜有爲') who had significant influence in Chosun, and whose Chinese-style interpretation/ translation of Western works would have harmonized the process of adopting Western knowledge amidst Chosun traditional thought.

■ REFERENCES

Daehanmaeil Shinbo (「大韓每日申報」).

Dokrib Shinmun (「독립신문」).

Hwangseong Shinmun (「皇城新聞」).

Ahn, Guk-Sun. 1908. "Issues for academic development: Political science - The need for political science research (興學講究: 政治學 政治學硏究의 必要)." *Gihoeheunghakhoe Wolbo*, No. 2.

Cho, Dong-Suk.1908. "National progress and the people's spirit (國家의 進步가 在國民精神)." *Daedonghakhoe Wolbo*, No. 3.

Daehangheunghakbo. 1909. "Academic Issues: Political theory (學藝 政治論)." No. 8.

Doo, Chun-Saeng. 1908. "The Origins of Law(法律發生의 原因)." *Daedonghakhoe Wolbo*, No. 1.

Han, Sang-Woo. 1909. "Educational section: The necessity of economics (敎育部: 經濟學의 必要라)." *Suhbukhakhoe Wolbo*, No. 17.

Kim, Ik-Yong. 1908. "Our present duties and rights in regards to the state (今日吾人의 國家에 대한 義務及權利)." *Suhbukhakhoe Wolbo*, No. 1.

Kwon, Bo-Sang. 1908. "Legal Studies (法律學)." *Daedonghakhoe Wolbo*, No. 1.

Lee, Gi. 1908a. "State theories (國家學說)." *Honamhakbo*, No. 1.

Lee, Myung-Jae. 1908b. "Academic issues: Economic theories (學海: 經

濟學說).” *Rakdongchinmokhoehakbo*, No. 4.

Moon, Sang-Woo. 1908a. “Academic issues: Principles of economics (學海: 經濟學原論).” *Sanghakgye*, No. 3.

Moon, Sang-Woo. 1908b. “Introduction to Commerce (商業通論).” *Sanghakgye*, No. 1.

Pubyul Dokseoin. 1908. “Classification of political systems (國體의 區別).” *Daedonghakhoe Wolbo*, No. 8.

Pubyul Dokseoin. 1909. “Types of companies and their characteristics (會社의 種類及性質).” *Daedonghakhoe Wolbo*, No. 12.

Ryu, Wan-Young. 1907. “Editorial: Law and economics – which is more important? (論說: 論法律과 經濟의 何者ㅣ 優勝).” *Bubjunghakgye*, No. 2.

Yoon, Guh-Hyun. 1907. “Commentary on production (生産을 論함).” *Gongsuhakbo*, No. 3.

Yoon, Hyo-Jung. 1906. “Non-patriotism of the people in an autocracy (專制國民無愛國思想論).” *Daehanjaganghoe Wolbo*, No. 5.

Yoon, Sung-Hee. 1908b. “Issues for academic development: Economics – Frugality and wastes (興學講究: 經濟學 吝嗇이 勝於濫費).” *Gihoeheunghakhoe Wolbo*, No. 2.

Yoon, Young-Jin. 1908a. “Issues for academic development: Advice on urgent duties of the people (興學講究: 勸告 國民急務).” *Gihoeheunghakhoe Wolbo*, No. 3.

Chung, Yong-Hwa. 2004. “The adoption and development of Western human rights (서구 인권사상의 수용과 전개).” In *The Adoption of Western Culture Modern Reform* (『서구문화의 수용과 근대개혁』). Seoul: Taehaksa.

Joo, Jin-Oh. 2004. “The formation and development of enlightened civilization theory in the late 19th century (19세기 후반 文明開化論의 형성과 전개)." In *The Adoption of Western Culture Modern Reform* (『서구문화의 수용과 근대개혁』). Seoul: Taehaksa, 2004.

Kang, Man-Gil. 1973. "Issues with commerce during the Great Korean Empire (大韓帝國 時期의 상공업 문제)." *Asia Yeongu*, No. 50.

Kim, Do-Hyung. 1994. *Research on Political Thought during the Korean Empire* (『大韓帝國期의 政治思想 研究』). Seoul: Jisik Sanupsa.

Kim, Do-Hyung. 2004. "The development of enlightened civilization theory during the early Korean Empire (大韓帝國 초기 文明開化論의 발전)." In *The Adoption of Western Culture Modern Reform* (『서구문화의 수용과 근대개혁』). Seoul: Taehaksa.

Kim, Dong-No. 1999. "The modernity of the enlightenment party intellectuals and modern transformation in late Chosun (한말 개화파 지식인의 근대성과 근대적 변혁)." *Asia Munhwa*, No. 14.

Kim, Dong-No. 2009. *Prelude to Modernity and Colonization* (『근대와 식민의 서곡』). Paju: Changbi.

Kim, Hyo-Jun. 2000. *Thoughts on the State in Modern Korea* (『근대 한국의 국가사상』). Seoul: Chulhak-gwa Hyunsilsa.

Lee, Seung-Ryul. 2007. *Empire and Merchants* (『제국과 상인』). Seoul: Yuksabipyungsa.

Lee, Tae-Jin. 2000. *Reinvestigating the Kojong Era* (『고종시대의 재조명』). Seoul: Taehaksa.

Oh, Young-Sup. 2004. "*The Trend of Awareness of International Law after Opening of the Ports* (개항후 만국공법 인식의 추이)." In *The Adoption of Western Culture Modern Reform* (『서구문화의 수용과 근대개혁』). Seoul: Taehaksa.

Shin, Yong-Ha. 1975. *A Study on the Independence Club* (『獨立協會研究』). Seoul: Iljogak.

Shin, Yong-Ha. 2010. *Intellectual History of Korean Enlightenment Thought and Movement* (『한국 개화사상과 개화운동의 지성사』). Paju: Jisik Sanupsa.

Suh, Young-Hee. 2003. *A Study on Political History of the Great Korean Empire* (『대한제국 정치사 연구』). Seoul: Seoul National University Press.

Wang, Hyun-Jong. 2003. *The Kabo Reform and the Formation of the Modern Korean State* (『한국 근대국가의 형성과 갑오개혁』). Seoul: Yuksabipyungsa.

Won, Jong-Gyu. 1991. *The History of Chosun Political Systems, Vol. 3* (『조선정치제도사 3』). Seoul: Baeksan Jahryohwon.

Giddens, Anthony. 1990. *The Consequences of Modernity*. Stanford: Stanford University Press.

Grieder, Jerome B. 1981. *Intellectuals and the State in Modern China*. New York: The Free Press.

Weber, Max. 1978. *Economy and Society*, edited by Guenther Roth and Claus Wittich. Berkeley: University of California Press.

CHAPTER 2.

Early Modernity and Social Science in Late Chosun Korea: Nation-State Sovereignty and the Role of Japan*

Sang-Sook Jeon, Duk-Kyu Jin**

Ⅰ. Introduction

Social science can be viewed both as a particular event in the history of Western modernization and as a broader part of the process of modern social change. It has thus been described as both the academic study of social behavior and as a body of thought direct linked with its own historical place and time (e.g. Bernal, 1984: 23-30; Hunt and Colandor, 1999:3; Muto, 2009: 23). Accordingly, the social science that spread to the East under Western expansion can be said to reflect particular aspects of the Western experience during the

* This paper was revised from the Korean version published in *Asia Yon'gu* (『아시아연구』), Volume 16, No.2, 2013.

** Sang-Sook Jeon(Research Professor), Duk-Kyu Jin(Visiting Professor), Institute of State Governance Studies, Yonsei University.

19th and early 20th century. It is this particular form of social science that East Asian countries embraced in their attempts to modernize in the face of Western powers.

In the case of Korea, encounters with various foreign powers led to the search for a self-reliant form of modernization. It was in these contexts that Korea came to adopt modern Western knowledge. However, this search for self-reliant modernization ultimately ended in failure with the loss of national sovereignty to the Japanese Empire. Following this, Korean adoption of Western knowledge came to be institutionalized, on one hand, in the modern education system of colonial Korea and, on the other, in the resistance movement against Japanese colonization. As a result, Korean social science is characterized by strong exogenous factors, in the sense that foreign Western knowledge was adopted as a means to escape the grips of foreign powers (Japan or otherwise). This foreign nature of Korean social science faced much criticism from those who instead argued for more endogenous or indigenous forms of knowledge (Moon, 1979). That being said, the adoption of foreign knowledge here also carries the implication of making this knowledge one's own. That is, it is important here to take into consideration the will of the agents adopting such knowledge. It is this process of critical assessment and contextualisation of knowledge that critics of the exogeneity of Korean social science sought to promote.

This work is grounded upon the above problem on the appropriateness of exogenous versus endogenous knowledge. Why does this issue seem to continuously arise? In order to better understand and engage with this issue, it may be worth investigating how Korean social science came to arise from the search for self-reliant modernization and embrace of modern learning. The resulting empirical evidence may help uncover the intellectual genealogy and particular characteristics of Korean social science during the modern and contemporary era, and shed light on the mutual relationship between Korean society and Korean social science research. A number of prior works have contributed towards this end. Jeon (2012b) presents a historical-political analysis of newspaper and magazine articles from the modern transition period to reveal the characteristics and critical thought on Western knowledge and social science. Jeon (2012c) then compares the form of civil society and civil liberties arising in social science articles with the form in which it arose in Korean society and individuals. Finally, Jeon (2012d) examines how Western social science was transformed as it was embraced in East Asia by examining Japan's adoption of German state science, which was selective employed again first in China and then in Korea.

Accordingly, the purpose of this study is to examine Korea's adoption of social science during its early transition to modernity up until colonization. It takes as a foundation a sizeable body of works including not only the aforementioned sources, but also prior work on the adoption of Western knowledge in Korea (Choi J.G., 1982; Ewha Womens University Korean Culture Research Institute, 2004, 2007; Ha Y.S., 2009; Jeon B.H., 1996; Kim D.H., 1994; Kim H.J., 1996, 2007, 2009; Kim H.J., 2000; Kim Y.G, 1997, 2008; Lee G.J., 1985; Lee W.J., 1998; Moon J.S., 1998; Park M.G., 2009; Park S.S., 2008).

Historical contexts reveal deep ties between social science, state development, and public issues of the times, which work to shape and develop on another.[1] Broadly speaking, the largest influence here was

---

[1] The English term 'social science' was first coined in 1846 through the English translation of August Comte's work (Boorstin, 1987: 15). However, it wasn't until the late 19th century that social science would become institutionalized as an independent de-

perhaps the historical and political legacy of the nation-state, which has very much shaped the present (Wagner et al., 1991: 5-7). The same holds in the contexts of Korean society and its respective adoption of social science. The critical factor considered here are the views of those key agents who constructed the modern Korean nation-state. The notion that Western ways were necessary in order to drive late modernization may be particularly important for the contexts of East Asia. This stance may help reveal the universal versus particular aspects to be found between Eastern and Western forms of modernization (Kang, 2013: 11-17). Accordingly, this work attempts to understand how the principal agents advocating modern nation-state reforms came to realize their aims through the process of adopting Western knowledge and social science.

In these contexts, this work attempts such comparative analysis within the specific contexts of Korean social science. It further offers a starting point for investigating the intellectual genealogy and characteristics of modern and contemporary Korean social science. It also holds significance in clarifying the historical contexts for formation and development of Korean social science during the ensuing colonial period. Finally, these findings may offer a glimpse into some of the general characteristics of Korean modernity.

---

partment(s) (Manicas, 1987: 193-212; Wallerstein, 1994: 29-31). The timing of this insitutionalizing additionally varies from country to country (Kim, 1995). In 19th and late 20th century Korea, awareness of social science as an academic discipline had not yet been established. Accordingly, this work attempts to deduce the early form of the social sciences, which may differ from the form that the generic term social science may refer to today.

II. Modern Social Science: The Intellectual Foundations of the 19th Century Western Nation-State System

As an academic field, social science addresses human society in its many and varied dimensions. Its role is to analyze and explain human values in socio-historical context in a scientific and systematic manner. Such descriptive elements also offer prescriptive insight on how such values affect social change. In this regard, the social sciences, more-so than the natural sciences, can be said to be directly linked with history (Bernal, 1984: 23-30).

This broader notion of social science has become something like common sense amongst the public today. The rise of this social science occurred in the backdrop of a secularizing modernity, driven by the development of the natural sciences. As is well known, the whole of Western learning, starting from philosophy, originates from Ancient Greece. Arguments on human society—the core domain of social science—is no exception. Many of the issues occupying Greek thinkers, such as the role of the Greek state (i.e. politics), the relationship between the human mind and society (i.e. psychology), or the relationship between the market and the individual (e.g. economics), continue to hold relevance in the social sciences today. Accordingly, the history of social science can be said to start with Ancient Greece (Hunt and Colander, 1999: 27). That being said, it was in the 19th century that social science would become the prevailing belief of an emerging modern world system powered by modern science, new technology, and mechanized civilization. During this time, the philosophical traditions of the Middle Ages also came to be institutionalized in the natural sciences, social sciences, and humanities. Here, social science was a sort of 'third culture' seated in between the natural sciences and the humanities (Wallerstein, 1994: 17-19). It was thus that Enlightenment era society and culture came to set the standards for historical and cultural development. It was further acknowledged that humans have changed and will continue to change. The resulting consciousness of the self and society furthered an awareness of social issues and promoted efforts to understand and resolve them. It is in this process that social science developed (Hunt and Colander, 1999: 28-29).

The 17th century Scientific Revolution and its fruits in Newtonian empirical science came to be viewed as endowing trustworthy method for shedding new light on the issues of human society. By the second half of the 18th century, these 'modern' scientific methods began being concertedly applied to social problems to generate solutions (Hamilton, 1978: 39). Premised upon a fundamental trust in human reason, such efforts utilized empirical methods to address social problems and solutions. These efforts constituted what came to be called social science. In following scientific principles, these efforts were premised upon the empirical verifiability of social issues.

This social science was formed in the contexts of states undergoing modernization during the 19th and 20th centuries. Urbanization, industrialization, and broader political and economic reorganization presented fertile grounds for wide-ranging empirical investigations. Amidst the consequent social issues faced by the state, social science came to play a central role in guiding state policy. In 18th and early 19th century Europe, this manifested in states' pursuit of policy science ('polizey-wissenschaaften') in order to understand and reform administrative regulations and policies. Although 'policy science', as a term, fell out of use by the second half of the 19th century, it can be seen as a forbearer to modern social science. During this period, politics became the specialized field for state administrators, sociology became the science of society, and economics began to establish multiple bodies of theory. Thus, when viewed in historical context, social science was shaped in various ways by the state development and social issues of its times. More specifically, these points influenced social science, such as the behavior of state organizations dictating state, individuals constituting said state organizations, and traditions and culture that, in turn, animated such individuals. Perhaps most important consideration of all, however, is the nation-state and its historical and political legacy—one which continues to manifest in the world we live in today (Wagner et al., 1991: 5-7).

Despite their national differences, European states—via their respective experiences of industrialization—shared an implicit premise regarding social science. This premise is that knowledge is empirical and quantitative. While this premise did not go uncontested, it, too, can be viewed as a product of European history or the Western experience (Wagner et al., 1991: 221). That is, it was grounded upon Western European faith in reason to produce a form of knowledge that was distinctively modern and Western-centric (Hamilton, 1978: 39).

Early Western social science thus viewed the social change sweeping across 19th century Europe as a 'normal' kind of change. Accordingly, social science was defined as an empirical field of research targeting the social world, with the purpose of influencing or otherwise affecting social change. This was a collective creation of individuals living in a particular place and time, seeking to achieve a particular purpose. The institutionalization of such knowledge was achieved via reform of the traditional European university structure, with the social processes of three subjects (i.e. state, market, individual) setting the disciplinary boundaries of three fields (i.e. politics, economics, sociology). This institutionalization of social science reflected the victory of liberalism, the dominant ideology of the capitalist world economy. The resulting theories on 'normal' social change only recognized the social change of civilized peoples as 'normal', and projected a need—or rather, a duty—for the civilized to bring about normal social change (i.e. Western modernization) unto uncivilized peoples. Social science, in order to normalize social change, became a means for intellectual world domination and a means to control social change (Wallerstein, 1994: 29-32).

In this way, social science has been, from the beginning, directly linked with the transformation of traditional society into a modern one. The focus on modern transformation can thus be viewed as a defining characteristic of social science. In other respects, however, social science can also be viewed as a product of the very modernization that it attempts to bring about. Thus, in the context of European empires, social science arose in response to the particular problems of modernization to serve as a foundation for rational and enlightened social order (Wagner et al., 1991: 2). Put more explicitly, social science provided intellectual foundations for the rise of the bourgeoisie—the leaders of capitalist industrialization—and the modern nation-state system.

III. The Selective Adoption of Social Science by Meiji Restoration Bureaucrats in Japan

Western social science entered East Asia as Western empires marched Eastwards. Equipped with modern arms and technology, these empires forced open 'uncivilized' countries in the East under the threat of naval guns and international law and offered means to introduce 'civilization'

(Jeon S.S., 2012b: 49, 2012c: 185). However, Eastern learning and knowledge was based on a different epistemic tradition than the West. In Eastern perspective, Western social science thus appeared foreign or alien. There was little continuity to be found between pre-existing social, political, and economic thought and this new Western science (Wagner et al., 1991: 221). However, the Opium Wars marked a turning point in Eastern sentiments, which faced the shocking reality that traditional Chinese civilization had been defeated by modern Western civilization. This so-called 'clash of civilizations' produced an intellectual reaction in China, as signified in the publication of the *Illustrated Treatise on the Maritime Kingdoms* ('해국도지' or '海國圖志'), which spearheaded efforts to inform Chinese of the world situation and to utilize achievements from the West in order to drive modern change.

Japan, in particular, was shocked by the outcome of the Opium War and the publication of the *Illustrated Treatise on the Maritime Kingdoms*. The former, which began to circulate in Japan in 1851, was particularly influential in intellectual society, and stimulated interest in military studies. Adding to this was the arrival of Perry's black ships in 1853, which concluded with Japan opening its doors, embracing the international law system, and adopting Western knowledge (and in particular, social science). After being overwhelmed by US naval power, Japan came to encounter Western international law and social science during subsequent trade and diplomatic negotiations—a turning point which is considered to have set Japan in the direction of modernization. The active embrace of international law came to strongly influence the orientation and policy direction of Meiji Restoration in 1868. The Meiji Restoration, which can be viewed as the origin of contemporary Japan, set the country in the direction of modernization and systematically adopted international law as a means to drive said modernization (Masao, 1973; Inoue, 1973: 2; Jang I.S., 2002: 202; Jeon S.S., 2012e: 280-283).

Japan, in the face of powerful and technologically advanced Western powers, acutely felt a sense of crisis with the prospects of losing national sovereignty. This arose not only through their forced opening, but also through the earlier defeat of China at the hands of modern Western powers and the resulting thought that there was no chance of winning face-to-face with the West. Japan chose to adapt to Western international law and the modern world system in order to seek a path towards modernization.

After the Peace of Westphalia, international law and its principle of the balance of power served as a political weapon for Western empires. However, it was also a system that non-Western countries—if they proved to be fast and adaptable enough—could utilize against Western powers (Jeon S.S., 2012b: 50-51). If one understood the operating principles of international law and adapted their stance accordingly, then the system guaranteed some minimal power and demands. Japan, amidst strained relations with the West, thus adopted international law in its search for ways to preserve its independence. Through desperate and strenuous effort, they aimed to achieve standing as a modern civilization superior to China and comparable to the West.

In the Westphalian system, the notion of state sovereignty is premised upon the conception of a state as an unified and independent actor; that is, unified internally and independent externally. While the principle of mutual reciprocity applied across those in the Westphalian system, it did not extend to those who belonged to outer regions. It is thus that Westphalian international law came to be both the source of Japan's national crisis and—through integration—a potential solution (Imai,

2003: 151-152).[2]

In Bakumatsu Japan, the adoption of Western knowledge spurred the related task of reshaping the intellectual foundations of Japanese cultural identity, with emphasis on the application and practice of thought. Amidst fluctuating domestic and foreign circumstances, Japan drove a great transformation in its fundamental worldview from that of the ancient Chinese classics and national studies to that of Western social science, spearheaded by international law. The form of Japanese social science that resulted was characterized by a pragmatism in efficiently driving social change. From the theory of national prosperity and defense (부국강병론) and the Tokugawa Shogunate of the Bakumatsu period, plans prioritized the creation of a strong and unified modern state over resistance against foreign power. New plans for state-building, furnished by the new ideas and intellectuals of the Bakumatsu period, attempted to sever ties with the old social order via the Meiji Restoration. Furthermore, Japan needed to realize a level of national prosperity and military power rivaling that of Western powers in order to secure recognition as a unified state and its associated sovereignty (Ishida, 2003: 45; Okita, 2007: 65-66, 106-107; Muto, 2009: 7; Jeon S.S., 2012c: 186-187).

Here, the bureaucrats and the plans behind the Meiji Restoration hold particular significant in understanding how Japan embraced Western social science in its own particular way. First are the Meiji bureaucrats who established a modern Japanese Imperial state that was on par with the wealth and powerful Western empires. Through the political crisis of 1881 (Meiji year 14), these bureaucrats, who started as patriots in the 'revere the emperor, expel the barbarians' movement ('Sonnō jōi'

---

[2] For more on the Westphalian system, see Kim D.S. (1998: 223-249).

or '尊皇攘夷'), were able to align with the modern state system, which upheld a strong monarchy as a symbol of the state. This Meiji government was able to establish policies on the National Assembly demanded by the civil liberties movement and to erect the foundations for a modern state. Critical here is the fact that Prussian-style military rule guided the direction on policy for the legislation of the Meiji constitution. The Meiji government, which had been on the defensive against a rising civil liberties movement, promised a national assembly and dampened the brunt of anti-government attacks, while simultaneously securing authority over the establishment of a constitutional system. This was the direct result of two major events. The first was the ousting of Ōkuma Shigenobu by members of the former Satsuma-Chōshū Alliance, who then gained complete control over the Meiji government. The second was the establishment of Ito Hirobumi, the lead figure behind this political upheaval, as the driver behind the political situation and the legislation of the constitution to follow (Kim C.R., 1973: 216-17). Accordingly, one could say that the political crisis of 1881 would come to regulate the content and characteristics of early Japanese social science.

The political crisis of 1881 derailed plans for the establishment of a modern nation-state from the Meiji Reformation and concluded with the victory of bureaucrats affiliated with German studies. Under their hegemony, Japanese social science came to develop an intellectual climate defined by German legal and political thought (Yamamuro, 1984: 250-280; Okita, 2007: 161). In 1871, after carrying out the abolition of the han system and establishment of the prefecture system ('廢藩置縣'), Meiji bureaucrats established a Ministry of Education to hold implement and administer a unified national education policy (Motoyama, 1998: 3-4). Following this, in September 1881, a German studies society was formed to promote German state science. In 1882, British law studies came to be replaced by national law studies at the University of Tokyo. In April 1883, the University of Tokyo established a department and professorship of German law, and additionally designates German as the sole second language. In 1886, all governmental and public schools were reorganized under new ordinates, with the imperial college placed at the top (Jeon, 2012c: 190-191). These policies endowed a modern Meiji state in which modern citizens did not yet exist with absolute imperial authority in order to overcome the crisis of national sovereignty. This authority was further institutionalized through the national school system, providing firm ground for the education of the modern citizen.[3]

The attempt by Meiji bureaucrats to establish a modern state to secure sovereignty also served as the process by which Western social science came to be selectively adopted. The studies of the Meiji state made no distinction between politics and public administration. Meiji bureaucrats argued that the intellectual wellspring of Western modernity needed to be identified and adapted to Japanese contexts in order to establish the modern state. It is in their preferred choice of German state science that one finds this characteristic unification or lack of separation between politics and public administration. 19th century German state science viewed state law and politics, centered on the state, as inseparable. The discipline of politics as found in the UK and the US fell under the broader discipline of state science of Germany. So too did state law (staatsrechtslehre) also fell under state science. For Meiji bureaucrats establishing a modern Japanese state, it was this German state science that answered to their needs. It was consequently institutionalized in Japanese education via

3 For reference to sovereignty and Japanese empire, see Jeon S.S. (2012c).

the establishment of the national school system. These form important and unique contexts that would be reflected in early Meiji social science. On the other hand, the adoption of UK and US social science, arising out of different histories of political and economic change, would lead to the subdivision of independent fields within social science and enable a blossoming of knowledge on state and society. However, this would not occur until the weakening of imperial sovereignty and the rise to power of the civil liberties movement towards the start of the Taisho period. Up until then, Japanese social science can be said to have developed within the contexts of state science, which held a central place in the Japanese national curriculum (Jeon S.S., 2012c: 191-192).[4] It was under the dominant influence of German state science, that the people ('volk') were first shaped into modern citizens; that is, principal agents to be held responsible for the nation.

While Western social science reflects the interests of the bourgeoisie who led capitalist industrialization and provided intellectual foundations for the modern nation-state system, the case of Japan is somewhat different. In Japan, Western social science was accepted to protect national sovereignty and to serve as an intellectual source to guide efforts to drive modern state reform by Meiji reformists and bureaucrats. Accordingly, early Japanese social science explicitly served the needs of Meiji bureaucrats seeking to establish the modern state. Similar to the words of Ishida Takeshi (石田雄), Japanese social science, characterized as imported and pragmatic, was shaped alongside the education system within the genealogy of German state science.

---

[4] For more on German state science, see Jellinek (1974), which further refers to the works of J.K. Bluntschili and G. Jellinek.

The purpose of importing knowledge was, again, connected with the practical demand of findings a way out of crisis. As a form of modern knowledge, Japanese social science arose from this crisis in the face of Western modernity as an intellectual foundation for the top-down construction of a modern Japanese nation-state. The development of Western social science reflects political and social changes in the West. Acting in reverse, the development of Japanese social science reflects the purpose of driving such political and social changes. Selectively transplanting and institutionalizing modern knowledge served to justify and realize for modern reforms. In this sense, Japanese social science was introduced and developed in line with clear political motives.

This kind of early Meiji social science, through a series of political events leading up to the February 1889 proclamation of the constitution of the Great Japanese Empire, contributed to the construction of the modern Meiji state. The highest priority here was to overcome the national crisis faced by its forced opening by Western powers. In order to face this crisis, German state science, which produced a monarchy endowed with absolute power under Frederick the Great, was selectively adopted to systemize top-down reforms. The Meiji constitution, which laid the basic framework for the Meiji state, seemed to reflect typical 19th century constitutional law in specifying the authority of the monarchy and National Assembly. However, given the much stronger authority endowed upon the monarchy, this resemblance did not go beyond external appearances (Kim C.R., 1993: 220). The particularities of the Meiji state and constitution can be said to be the result of Japanese social science and, at the same time, representative of Japanese social science. That is, Japanese social science can, on one hand, be viewed from Western standards as possessing the minimal essential criteria of being 'modern';

that is, similar to Western social science. On the other hand, selective adoption and pragmatic contextualization produced a social science that took on a very particular Japanese form.

This Japanese social science, according to Masao Maruyama, would perfect the new Japanese state to include both the openness of modern Western society and, at the same time, a distinct and unified identity in international contexts (Masao, 1961: 9-10). By informing the direction of the Meiji state, early Japanese social science provided both intellectual foundations for the ideal Japanese imperial state and political thought for its realization. It further answered to the demands of Japanese society, which had not yet established the concepts of the modern state and sovereignty (Jeon, 2012c: 204-205). Social science in Meiji Japan thus served to guide the construction of a modern state and to justify foreign expansion in the name of national interest or national strength. At the same time, Japanese social science was also highly influential as an intellectual wellspring, in turn, for Chinese and Korean intellectuals, who similarly sought to modernize in defense against Western powers.[5]

Thus, Meiji social science contributed to domestic unification around monarchical authority and helped spur reforms to establish a modern Japanese state. However, such states saw regions lying outside the Westphalian system as subject to legitimate attempts to extend the reach of state sovereignty (i.e. imperial expansion). Thus, while Chinese and Korean intellectuals saw in Japanese social science a successful model for overcoming their mutual national crises, this social science was also highly influenced by the thought of Frederick the Great. That is, Japanese

[5] For the Japanese adoption of German state science and its influence in Korea and China, see Jeon S.S. (2012c), Ch.3–4.

social science also carried within it the rationale and justification that would serve Japanese imperial expansion. As seen in the debates on Junghan theory ('정한론' or '征韓論' or 'せいかんろん') during early Meiji on the conquest of Korea, this body of thought could have also been perceived as a threat by Japan's neighbours. However, Korean intellectuals failed to identify this danger and were only able to see Japanese social science as an intellectual wellspring for modernization.

IV. Civil Liberties versus Royal Authority and Japan's Influence in the Adoption of Western Social Science

The incorporation of Korea into the modern international system and the introduction of Western international law began in earnest with the forced opening of Chosun by Japan. Korea, which had previously avoided direct contact with the West, was unable to defy the currents of modern internationalization after its opening. Consequently, international law came to be actively embraced in order to understand contemporary realities and learn from the modernization and intellectual foundations of Japan.

The first Western scholarship introduced to Korea was in the early 17th century via China. These were the writings of Western missionaries active in China, which were imported by Korean public officials and intellectuals visiting there. The Korean translations of these writings were influential to scholars in the Realist School of Confucianism ('실학파'), who recognized the rationality of this Western scholarship and even proposed a theoretical approach for accommodating such knowledge ('서학수용론'). However, this accommodation of Western knowledge was severely limited by Korea's subsequent closed-door policy and eventually relegated to a mere intellectual curiosity (Choi J.G., 1982: 18-20, 1990: 67; Lee T.J., 1997: 75; Lee W.S., 1979: 138-144, 1992: 135). This early knowledge, however, would later become influential again as a foundation for incoming Western knowledge after Chosun's opening. The Western knowledge that did arrive in Chosun via China was imported quite rapidly. For example, the *Illustrated Treatise on the Maritime Kingdoms* ('해국도지' or '海國圖志'), first published in China in December 1844, was introduced to Chosun in March 1845 through vice-minister ('호조참판') Kwon Dae-Geung ('권대긍' or '權大肯'). Another example, that of Lee Jung-Jik ('이정직' or '李定稷'), reveals some of the breadth of the knowledge imported from China. Lee, who attended the 1868 government mission to Peking and returned to Korea after studying modern sciences ('신학문'), wrote a piece on "An Outline of Kantian Philosophy" ('강씨철학설대략' or '康氏哲學設大略') before Kantian philosophy was even introduced to the Chinese (Yeungnam University National Culture Research Institute, 2000: 460-461).[6]

The *Illustrated Treatise on the Maritime Kingdoms* ('해국도지' or '海國圖志') and the *Illustrated Atlas of the World* ('영환지략' or '瀛環志略'), which contributed to a paradigm shift in China after the Opium Wars, also became required reading for Korean intellectuals. While these served guiding roles in expanding worldly knowledge during the times,

---

[6] PARK Jong-Hong was the first to make use of the term 'philosophy' ('철학'), even prior to the 1912 work on the history of Western ancient philosophy introduced here (*Godaeheehrabchul* ['고대희랍철' or '古代希臘哲學攷辯'] by philosopher LEE In-Jae ['이인재' or '李寅梓']). Accordingly, Park can be considered as the pioneering researcher on Western philosophy in Chosun (이광래, 2003: 225-226).

the closed-door policy significantly restricted the circulation of Western knowledge. Thus, Korean translations of new Western knowledge were not enough to connecting domestic political and social discussions with the larger unfolding realities of contemporary world affairs. Even as Korea was sending envoys ('문안사' or '問安使') to a defeated China post-Opium Wars, it failed to expand its global outlook. This reflected a sort of colour-blindedness in Korea's regards to the international situation. The continued adoption of a Sino-centric system and the failure to recognize the international negotiations it was already a part of make clear the country's limited frame of awareness (Jeon S.S., 2012e: 280-283; Lee, H.G., 1980: 204; Lee S.K., 1977: 142, 144).[7]

Korea, which failed to recognize the significance of the *Illustrated Treatise on the Maritime Kingdoms* or the use of international law, came to be forced open by Japan that recognized the significance of it and the usage of international law then came to succeed in modernizing. This is significant for understanding Korean modernity, its adoption of Western knowledge, and its early form of social science. Like Japan, Korea also adopted Western knowledge in the face of a possible loss of sovereignty at the hands of Western imperialism. However, Korea would not adopt its intellectual foundations directly from the West and instead adopted modern scholarship through Meiji Japan, which was viewed as a successful case of East Asian modernization.

After its opening, a 60-person Korean inspection team led by 12 experts ('신사유람단' or '紳士遊覽團') was sent to Japan to acquire the latest in modern knowledge. Following this was a proposal to send Korean students to study in Japan from the incoming Japanese minister

---

7 For the Chosun ruling class' awareness of the Opium War, see Ha J.S. (1998).

to Korea, Inoue Kaoru ('井上馨'), who was entrusted with the mission of establishing a new Korean system after victory in the Sino-Japanese War. In July 1895, 182 students were dispatched, followed by a second group of 64 students in 1897. It is not difficult to imagine that Japan's aim of this large scale government dispatch of students to Japan pointed to the formation of pro-Japanese bureaucrats and citizens in Korean society (Ahn Y.J., 1998: 133; *Chinmokhoehoebo*, 1895; Kim Y.M., 1981: 420-424; Lee T.J., 1997: 92). Along with Japan's victory after the Sino-Japanese War, the increasing number of students sent abroad increased Japan's domestic influence in Korea. While there were around 200 students studying in Japan in 1895, this would increase to more than 500 after the 1904–5 Russo-Japanese War (Abe, 1974; Lee G.R., 1986: 63).

These students educated in Japan are known for their leading roles in the Gapsin Coup ('갑신정변') and the Gabo Reforms ('갑오개혁'). Particularly post-Gabo Reforms, these former students applied and introduced Japanese knowledge adopted from the West in newspapers and magazines. From October 1895 onwards, *The Reunion Bulletin* ('친목회회보') began publication under the alumni association of these Japan-educated Koreans. Hanseong Newspaper('한성순보' and '한성주보') included works on social science and on reform policies. These, together with *The Independent* ('독립신문'), published since 1896 by Suh Jae-Pil ('서재필') who had studied in the US, and the *Hwangseong Newspaper*, published since 1898, formed the foundations for modern Korean social science.

From another perspective, the adoption of Western international law in open-door Chosun evidences a choice of Western over Eastern civilization. This demonstrated a departure from a traditional Sino-centric worldview. This change in worldview struck like lighting after the attempted modern reforms of Chosun society and the start of the Sino-Japanese War.[8] The vacuum left by the end of Sino-centric thought was filled by Japanese influence. In this way, Sino-centrism came to meet its end alongside increased dependence on Japan.

In the face of external threat, Chosun faced an internal conflict between those who advocated a policy of expulsion of foreign influence and those who advocated enlightenment reform. Adaption to the new international system necessarily entails changes to the domestic system. However, such changes were resisted by advocates of expulsion, who largely carried the interests of the ruling class. This conflict carried through even after Chosun's opening in the political struggle between reformist versus conservative forces. This conflict also carries through into the international dimension. Those advocating expulsion had the incumbent Sino-centric worldview, while those advocating modern reform affiliated with Japan. Amidst this conflict, Korean government, came to recognize the notions of 'balance of powers' and 'self-reliance' through texts such as *Chosun strategy* ('조선책략') *and Yieon* ('이언' or '易言'). It thus pursued, as part of its anti-Japan policy ('비아항일책' or '備我抗日策'), independent and direct negotiations with the US and other world powers (Ha Y.S., 2009: 219-220; Jeon S.S., 2012b: 54; Kim K.T., 1975: 201; Kim S.M., 2002). Similarly, stimulating the sense of crisis to China, which traditionally had a big influence, was also necessary in order to change Chinese views on Korea as a vassal state. As a result, the end of Sino-centric views was expedited and the Korean Empire leaned more

8 For more on the end of Korea's Sino-centric worldview in the contexts of East Asian international relations, see Kim and Jeon (2013: Ch.2).

towards Japan and Russia, which were locked in a confrontational relationship. This latter relationship was the results of Japan's northward continental expansion policy coming into direct conflict with Russia's southward expansion policy. Domestically, pro-monarchy conservatives and pro-civil liberties reformists both utilized and prolonged this tense international situation. The Russo-Japanese War would finally end the influence of Sino-centric views, which had already been in decline since the Sino-Japanese War, and spell victory for the enlightenment party.

The most important aspect sought after from Western social science was the way to modernize, similar to the West. If Korea was to preserve its sovereignty and become a wealthy and powerful country, it would need to acquire the intellectual foundations that enabled the same in the West. The modern Western political system, which reflected the wealth and power of the West, symbolized modern reform, was thus viewed as the highest priority. Though capitalist industrialization and the bourgeoisie, empowered by scientific advances, had led the Western nation-state system, it was the immediate threats of this modern political system that Eastern countries now faced. Thus, interest focused on the modern state and international law system of Western powers, who emphasized the need to implement open-door policies. Accordingly, the selective adoption of Western knowledge for modernization focused on social science (Jeon and Noh, 2013b: 88-89).

Despite the impetus for modernization after forced opening, the methods and political parties driving modernization were divided and in continuous conflict. Thus, the direction of reforms also changed in accordance with the changing political influence of those driving modernization. For example, one articles from the *Hwangseong Newspaper* ('황성신문' or '皇城新聞') advocated the adoption of Western knowledge together with the Realist school of Confucianism ('실학') and traditional civilization. Another approach from the political sphere unfolded in the Gwangmu Reforms' attempts to drive systematic modernization from the top-down. However, annexation by Japan would cause subsequent attempts at modern reform and the adoption of social science to unfold in the mode of colonial transplantation.

In these contexts, examining the substantive content of social science from opening up until annexation reveals the following. After Chosun's forced opening, the content introduced via social science was mainly related to modern politics and modern political reforms. Accordingly, an overwhelming volume of works on political science can be observed from this period.

Interest in political science arose in order to secure sovereignty as a modern state and to become a fully-fledged member of international society. Urgency only increased after the Second Japan-Korea Treaty of November 1905, which downgraded Korea to a protectorate. Research reflecting the political challenges of a protectorate began to proliferate, along with interest in law (Bubjunghakgye, 1909). For example, May 1905 marks the establishment of a dedicated research society on constitutional governance and the beginnings of institutionalized law education (Hwangseong Shinmun, 25 May 1905). As political reform to break through the sovereign crisis was the highest priority, most emphasis was placed constitutional governance. For example, constitutional governance was described as "the common body of the royalty and the people. Accordingly, decisions on public affairs depended on consensus between top and bottom and the operational foundations lay in the political parties and political assemblies chosen by the people" (Ahn G.S., 1908; Yoon H.J., 1906).[9] It is worth noting that this description reflects less Western parliamentary government and more the Japanese privy council (Jeon S.S., 2012b: 58-62; Joo J.O., 1995: 185; Lee T.J., 1997: 114-115).

The reason behind the Korean Empire's choice of constitutional monarchy lay in its offer of real sovereignty. Sovereignty, which determines national competitiveness and strengthens internal stability (e.g. self-reliance, independence), was viewed as the key to overcoming the impasse faced as a protectorate state (*Daedonghakhoewolbo*, 1908a; Lee G.J., 1907). However, a problem arose in that the monarchy proclaimed the Korean Empire in order to strengthen royal authority. In light of the chaotic political situation that arose after suddenly halting Gabo Reforms, it was argued that what was needed was a weakening and not a strengthening of royal authority. Viewing the monarchy as representative of the state was critiqued as a relic of autocratic politics (*Dahanjaganghoewolbo*, 1906; Lee G.J., 1907). Yet, while mentions of a republic are made, no insistence is made on the abolishment of monarchy (Choi S.H., 1906: 1; *Daedonghakhoewolbo* 1908b; Won Y.H., 1908: 1).

While state-led modern reforms began with the proclamation of the Korean Empire, intellectuals who embraced modern knowledge after the opening of Chosun wanted to restrict royal authority—though not to the point of advocating a republic, which would disavow the Imperial system of modernized Meiji Japan. Rather, they advocated the strengthening of civil liberties, and came to influence the directions of enlightenment reforms after Korea's opening.[10] After opening and the rise of young elites and bureaucrats under the influence of Japan, the top-down attempt of

[9] Original text as follows: "君民同體이며 上 下一 致로 萬機를 公議에 의하여 결행하는데 在하니 그 운용 기초는 國 民多數의 선량 公黨公會에 在"

[10] For more on the awareness of civil liberties in late Chosun, see Jeon S.S. (2012c).

the Gabo Reforms were cut off by the proclamation of the Korean Empire and the Gwangmu Reforms. However, just as the Gabo Reforms returned reformists who had been pushed out by the Gapsin Coup ('갑신정변') back to the fore of politics, the downgrading of Korea into a Japanese protectorate provided a space for these reformists once again to resume their plans. Monarchy and royal reforms became viewed as the failed reforms of incompetent leaders that led to Korea becoming a protectorate state. In reality, the Korean Empire, which stressed royal authority, and Japan, which argued the protectorate as a means to exercise real authority, formed a dual power structure. In this situation, those who strongly advocated civil liberties were also arguing for a weakening of royal authority. The conflict that continued on since forced opening between conservatives and reformists was reflected in this present situation between the strengthened royal authority of the Korean Empire and the call for civil liberties based on foundations provided by Western social science.

The constitutional government and constitutional monarchy being advocated bore in mind Japan's privy council. The theory being applied here was state theory or, more specifically, the organic state theory of Johann Caspar Bluntschli's organic state theory adopted in Japan. That the Korean Empire also utilized Bluntschli's theory has already been documented (Jeon B.D., 1974). This was due to views that the enhancement of state competitiveness would be beneficial for reforms establishing vital state sovereignty.

At this time, voices that accepted the loss of sovereignty as a protectorate began to arise formally here and there. Rather than politics, law, and other studies for the training of government officials, which had little use amidst lost sovereignty, it was better to focus on studies that would raise industrial and economic skills (*Daehanmaeil Shinbo*, 21

January 1909). Insistence on policies for promoting industry and production arose from many quarters (Joh J.E., 1906: 11-12; Byun Y.M., 1907: 12; Lee B.I., 1907: 2- 4; Daehanmaeil Shinbo, 1907.10.25.). This, alongside demands for commercial knowledge, spurred a call for economic research. Western economics began to be introduced in earnest in the 1900s after Korea became a protectorate. Along with the notions of strenuous effort and industrial production, economics was institutionalized through education (Lee G.J., 1985: 58). The downgrading of Korea into a protectorate and the resulting awareness of the loss of sovereignty weakened the prospects of modern political reform and resulted in a search for policies to promote strenuous efforts and skills training.

On the other hand, views on Japan's intents—traditionally considered to be amicable—were awakened to reality, and triggered the shaping of a national consciousness. The theories of tripartite cooperation ('삼국협력론') and Asian solidarity ('아시아연대론'), which had previously been taken at face value, were now recognised as mere justification for deceitful policies (*Hwangseong Shinmun*, 1 March 1904). Similarly, Japan's talk of protection was recognized as hiding a path towards a vassal state (*Hwangseong Shinmun*, 3 October 1904). Consequently, the term 'nation' ('민족'), which had been often used in Korean translations of foreign texts, came to be reinterpreted as a modern concept. Thus began studies on national history and on the national community existing on the Korean peninsula. Nevertheless, the intellectual foundations for this research and awareness emerged under the influence of Japanese state science, which adopted Bruntschili's organic state theory, and was again reinterpreted by Liang Qichao (Jeon S.S., 2012c). Amidst the realities of a protectorate state, it was not possible to adopt such knowledge in a practical manner that was free from strong Japanese influence.

Thus, losing sovereignty as a protectorate also triggered a growing awareness of the concept of the modern nation and nationalism. These became concretely established in the thought of anti-Japanese independence movement after the 1910 annexation and colonialization by Japan. At the same time, social science would come to be institutionalized under Japanese colonization in the modern education system.

V. Conclusion

19th century Western social science served the interests of the governing system by providing justification for particular social changes through the systemization of academic scholarship and reasoning. Amidst these social changes, this scholarship reflected the interests of a new and rising modern ruling class. However, after the establishment of a governing system under this new ruling class, the interests of those that seized power was also subject to the unfolding of modernity. Consequently, modern social science can be said to reflect the driving forces behind modernization and the interests of the ruling class, which in turn changed with modernization.

After its encounters with the West, the East had little choice but to enact modern reforms, which were viewed as critical for protecting national sovereignty. Social science was viewed as providing the intellectual foundations for realizing modernization in pre-modern societies. Consequently, Western social science was selectively adopted and transposed in newly-opened countries in accordance to the form of modern reforms pursued by their ruling parties at the time. Thus, this phenomenon in which knowledge both reflected and serviced the ruling powers at the time can be seen as a universal characteristic of early modern social science.

In East Asia, early social science was imported as an intellectual foundation for the reform or revolution of pre-modern governing systems. Thus, knowledge from Western social science was selectively transplanted according to the conceptions of modernization held by the main agents of reform. This employment of knowledge for their practical benefits is a common characteristic of both Western and early Eastern social science. The early social sciences observed across countries exhibit diverse characteristics that were shaped by their respective historical contexts and their principal actors.

Japan, in its face-to-face confrontation with the West, learned from the failures of the Chinese experience. Under a heightened awareness of national crisis, it selectively adopted Western social science in its search for a solution. Western modernity, represented by international law, thus served as both the source of national crisis and the ideal model for realizing modern state sovereignty in the East. This ideal model was successfully realized under Meiji bureaucrats, who established a modern Japanese state after the Meiji Restoration. The German state science selected by bureaucrats was employed in establishing a Japanese constitutional monarchy that was operated by elder statesmen and Meiji bureaucrats. The selective utilization of 19th century German state science produce a form of social science with particular Japanese characteristics. That is, the adoption of select German legal philosophies set the contexts in which Japanese social science came to develop. Early Japanese social science was also institutionalized for the sake of shaping a national citizenry that did not exist prior to the Meiji state. A strong education system was needed to form national citizens who could act as representatives of a modern nation-state. Accordingly, Meiji social science did not separate politics and administration, and further viewed law and politics as inseparable. Finally, Meiji social science applied Frederick the Great's theory of absolute monarchy to achieve strong internal unification around the monarchy, as the representative of national sovereignty. Externally, this also served imperial plans to expand into foreign territories to expand national interests and power.

As seen earlier, Korean circumstances before and after its forced opening stood in distinct contrast with Japan, which foresaw the oncoming dangers through the Opium War and successfully came to establish a modern Meiji state. In Korea, political leaders were able to recognize the inescapability of country opening, but were unable to formulate a response. One reason was the greater influence of Japan which made open the country. Another is the continued conflict between governing powers after opening and their inability to overcome their divisions. The result is that reform efforts came to end with the Korea becoming a protectorate of an expansionary Japan (Jeon, 2012a). Since the publication of the *Hanseong Newspaper* ('한성순보' and '한성주보'), a variety of newspapers and magazines have introduced Western social science into Korean society.[11] These link with the attempts to realize modern reforms in the state. As social science was viewed as providing intellectual foundations to guide effective modern reforms, intellectuals and governing powers utilized such knowledge in various ways.

Under the influence of Japan, diverse works from modern Western social science were discussed and taught through the newly established

---

[11] For more on the subsequent introduction and adoption of social science in newspapers and magazines of the times, see Jin D.G. (2012) and Jeon S.S. (2011, 2012b).

modern school system. All shared in the aim of executing modern reforms resembling those in the West in order to establish a modern sovereign state. The necessity of modern reform was the major prerequisite to the establishment of state sovereignty. However, the factionalization of ruling powers prevented the establishment and unification of energies in any one particular orientation towards reform. Here, the long-term northbound continental expansion policy for Japan's modern state development had a significant effect in influencing the opening, downgrading as a protectorate, and eventual annexation of Korea. Efforts for self-reliant modernization withered under Japanese regulation and, combined with the inability to overcome conflicts between governing powers, resulted in the inability to drive modern reform.

Prior to annexation, Western social science was adopted in Korea with the clear aim of establishing a modern state. After its forced opening and under strengthened Japanese influence, however, this adoption of Western knowledge took an indirect path through Japan. It was thus difficult for Koreans to directly and independently interpret and adopt Western modernity and its intellectual foundations. The choice of Western social science was due to its perceived necessity for realizing modern reforms and subsequent state sovereignty. In this respect, early Korean social science shares with Japan its imported characteristics with an emphasis on producing practical value. It differs, however, in that the Korean adoption of Western modernity and social science was done indirectly through Japan.

As a result, the adoption of Western knowledge followed the Japanese style, which was recognized as a successful case of modernization. The threat of Japan to Korea arose from Japan's long-term plans regarding the necessity of constructing a modern Eastern state, via self-reliant modernization, against the backdrop of expanding Western imperialism. The indirect adoption of Western knowledge via Japan also led to the acceptance of the scholarly justifications underlying Japan's political plans. As social science has particularly close ties with shaping one's worldview, the development of social science was also influential in shaping the modern Korean state. Additionally, indirect adoption of Western social science without clearly recognizing its particular historical, political, and social contexts also led to problems in adopting its concepts to the contexts of an opened Chosun.

In this way, the content of early Korean social science adopted from opening up until annexation was systematized during colonization alongside the establishment of a modern national education system and the project of constructing a Japanese citizenry. On the other side, it was developed alongside Korean nationalism, forming intellectual foundations for the anti-Japanese national independence movement and the aim of establishing a modern Korean nation-state.

■ REFERENCES

Abe, Hiroshi. 1974. "Late Chosun Students Studying Abroad in Japan: An archival study 1, 2, 3 (舊韓末의 日本留學 -資料的考察 1, 2, 3)." *Han*, 3–5.

Ahn, Gook-Sun. 1908. "Heunghakganggu-The need for political science research (興學講究-정치학 연구의 필요)." *Gihoheunghakwolbo*, 2.

Bernal, J.D. 1984. *The History of Science, Vol. 4: The history of social science* (『과학사 4권 사회과학의 역사』). Translated by Jung-Ho Park. Seoul: Hanul.

Boorstin, Daniel J. 1987. *Hidden History*. New York: Vintage Books.

Bubjunghakgye. 1909. "Editorial: A lawyer's historical knowledge (논설: 법률가의 역사적 지식)." Issue 22.

Chinmokhoehoebo. 1895. "Miscellaneous news (雜報)." Issue 1.

Choi, Jong-Go. 1982. *The History of Korean Adoption of Western Law* (『한국의 서양법수용사』). Seoul: Pakyoungsa.

Choi, Jong-Go. 1990. *The History of Korean Law Studies* (『한국법학사』). Seoul: Pakyoungsa.

Dahanjaganghoewolbo. 1906. "Miscellaneous records: Distinguishing the state from the royal family (잡록: 國家及皇室의 分別)." Issue 3.

Daedonghakhoewolbo. 1908a. "The characteristics of sovereignty (통치권의 성질)." Issue 7.

Daedonghakhoewolbo. 1908b. "Different forms of government (政體의 구별)." Issue 8.

Dongrib Shinmun. "Editorial (론설)." 7 April 1899.

Ehwa Womens University Korean Culture Research Institute. 2004. *Adoption and Change in the Intellectual Concepts of Modern Enlightenment* (『근대계몽기 지식개념의 수용과 그 변용』). Seoul: Somyung Choolpan.

Ehwa Womens University Korean Culture Research Institute. 2007. *Shifts and Intensification towards Reality in Modern Enlightenment Knowledge* (『근대계몽기 지식의 굴절과 현실적 심화』). Seoul: Sohwa.

Ha, Jung-Shik. 1998. "The invasion of China by Western powers and Chosun's response (구미열강의 중국침략과 조선의 반응)." *Dongyanghak*, 28, 1–17.

Ha, Young-Sun. 2009. *History of the Conceptual Formation of Social Science in Modern Korea* (『근대한국의 사회과학 개념 형성사』). Seoul: Changjak-gwa Bipyungsa.

Hamilton, Peter. 1978. "The Historical Emergence of Social Science." In *Social Science and Social Change*. Milton Keynes: The Open University Press.

Hashikawa, Bunsou. 1971. *Intellectual History of Modern Japan 1* (『近代日本政治思想史 1』). Tokyo: Yoobigak.

Hunt, Elgin F. and David C. Colander. 1999. *Social Science: An Introduction to the Study of Society*. Boston: Allyn Bacon.

Hwangseong Shinmun. "Korea-Japan Treaty Negotiations (論韓日協商條約)." 1 March 1904.

Hwangseong Shinmun. "Another Warning (又警告)." 3 October 1904.

Imai, Hiromichi. 2003. "The legal structure of the Meiji state's emergency powers (긴급권국가로서의 '메이지국가'의 법구조)." *Bubsahakyeongu*, 27, 139-163.

Inoue, Isao. 1973. *Modern Japanese Intellectual History* (『近代日本思想

史』). Tokyo: Yoobigak Ssangsuh.

Ishida, Takeshi. 2003. *Japanese Social Science* (『일본의 사회과학』). Translated by Young-Hye Han. Seoul: Sohwa.

Jellinek, G. *General State Law* (『一般國法學』). Translated by Ashibe, Abe, Ishimura. Tokyo: Hakyang Suhbang.

Jeon, Bok-Hee. 1996. *The Theory of Social Evolution and National Thought* (『사회진화론과 국가사상』). Seoul: Hanul Academy.

Jeon, Bong-Duk. 1974. "The Establishment and Basic Thought of the Royal Constitution of the Korean Empire (대한국국제의 제정과 기본 사상)." *Bubsahak Yeongu,* 1, 1–20.

Jeon, Sang Sook. 2011. "The critical thought and characteristic traits of early Korean social science, as seen through the compilation of a literature database (문헌 DB 구축을 통해서 본 한국 초기 '사회과학'의 문제의식과 특성)." In *Proceedings of the 2011 SSK Conference on Key Actors and Critical Thought in the Adoption of Early Modern Social Science.*

Jeon, Sang Sook. 2012a. *Politics of the Chosun Governor General: The 'Relative Autonomy' of the Chosun Governor General and the Characteristics of Japan's Korean governance policy* (『조선총독 정치연구: 조선총독의 '상대적 자율성'과 일본의 한국지배정책 특질』). Paju: Jisik Sanupsa.

Jeon, Sang Sook. 2012b. "The historical nature of the adoption of modern 'social science', as seen through late Chosun newspapers and magazines: Critical thought and characteristics in the formation of early Korean 'social science' (한말 신문 · 잡지 언설을 통해 본 근대 서양 '사회과학' 수용의 역사적 성격: 한국 초기 '사회과학' 형성의 문제의식과 특성)." *Damron 201,* 15(2), 45–80.

Jeon, Sang Sook. 2012c. "Study on conceptions of 'individual' and 'society' in Korean society, as seen through late Chosun awareness of 'civil liberties': Perspectives on 'the people' and 'civil rights' in late Chosun news media on social science (한말 '민권' 인식을 통해 본 한국 사회의 '개인'과 '사회' 인식에 대한 원형적 고찰: 한말 사회과학적 언설에 나타난 '인민' 관과 '민권' 인식을 중심으로)." *Hangukjungchiwehgyosa Nonchong,* 33(2), 5–33.

Jeon, Sang Sook. 2012d. "East Asian adoption of modern 'social science' and the characteristics of Meiji Japan's 'social science': The adoption of Bruntschli's state science (근대 '사회과학'의 동아시아 수용과 메이지 일본 '사회과학'의 특질 : 블룬칠리 국가학 수용을 중심으로)." *Ehwa Sahak Yeongu,* 44, 181–220.

Jeon, Sang Sook. 2012e. "Confucian intellectuals and their 'modern' awareness and understanding of Western 'social science': The enlightened awareness and theory of Western learning of Kim Yoon, before and after the opening of Chosun (유교 지식인의 '근대' 인식과 서구 '사회과학'의 이해: 개국 전후 김윤식의 개화 인식과 서양학문수용론을 중심으로)." *Sahoe Yiron,* 42, 275–308.

Jeon, Sang Sook and Sang-Gyun Noh. 2013. "The Korean government's modern education system reforms and national schools before annexation (병합 이전 한국정부의 근대적 교육체제 개혁과 관학)." *Dongyangjungchisasangsa,* 12(1), 87–107.

Jin, Duk-Gyu. 2012. *The Intellectual Genealogy of Korean Social Science Research and Plans for the Founding of Korean Social Science Theory, Anthology I* (『한국 사회과학 연구의 지적 계보와 한국적 사회과학 이론 정립의 방안 자료집 I』). Seoul: Yonsei University Institute of State Governance Studies.

Ju, Jin-Oh. 1995. "The structure and formation of enlightenment reform theory in the latter half of the 19th century: The independence association (19세기 후반 개화 개혁론의 구조와 전개-독립협회를 중심으로).” PhD Dissertation, Yonsei University.

Jung, In-Sung. 2002. *International Political Thought of the Place: Yokoi Shonan and Kim Yoon-Sik on East Asia's Period of Changing Order* (『장소의 국제정치사상: 동아시아 질서변동기의 요코이 쇼난과 김윤식』). Seoul: Seoul National University Press.

Kang, Jung-In. 2013. *The Identity of Political Science: For the Sake of an Independent Korean Political Science* (『정치학의 정체성: 한국 정치학의 주체성을 위하여』). Seoul: Cheksehsang.

Kim, Chang-Rok. 1993. “The formation of modern Japanese thought on constitutional law (근대일본 헌법사상의 형성).” *Bub-gwa Sahoe*, 7, 1, 210–236.

Kim, Dae-Soon. 1998. “Surveying the development of the international community: From the Peace of Westphalia to the present (국제 공동체의 전개과정 개관: 웨스트팔리안 평화조약에서 현재 까지).” *Bubhak Yeungu*, 8, 223–249.

Kim, Do-Hyung. 1986. “The political science research of the late Chosun enlightenment movement (한말 계몽운동의 정치론 연구).” *Hanguksa Yeungu*, 54, 75–137.

Kim, Do-Hyung. 1994. *Research on Political Thought during the Korean Empire* (『대한제국기의 정치사상연구』). Seoul: Jishiksan Upsa.

Kim, Hak-Joon. 2000. *The Adoption of Western Political Science in Late Chosun* (『한말의 서양정치학 수용연구』). Seoul: Seoul National University Press.

Kim, Hyo-Jun. 1996. *The Early Adoption of Western Constitutional Theory* (『서양 헌법이론의 초기수용』). Seoul: Chulhak-gwa Hyunshilsa.

Kim, Hyo-Jun. 2007. *National Thought in Modern Korea* (『근대 한국의 국가사상』). Seoul: Chulhak-gwa Hyunshilsa.

Kim, Hyo-Jun. 2009. *Constitutional Law* (『헌법』). Seoul: Sohwa.

Kim, Kyung-Il. 1995. "Overcoming universalism and the Westernism in modern science: Wallerstein's historical social science (근대과학의 '보편주의'와 서구중심주의를 넘어서: 윌러스타인의 역사사회과학을 중심으로)." *Changjak-gwa Bipyung*, 89, 359–383.

Kim, Kyung-Tae. 1975. "Developments in the amendments and negotations of the unfair treaty: The Japanese 'national problem' in postwar 1880s (불평등조약 개정교섭의 전개: 1880년대 전후의 대일 '민족문제')." *Hanguksa Yeungu,* 11, 165-204.

Kim, Joo-Sam. 2009. "An analysis of Chinese and Japanese strategic directions arising from the Opium War and East Asian modernisation (아편전 쟁과 동아시아 근대화과정에서 나타 난 중, 일의 대응방식 분석)." *Asiah Yeungu*, 11-3.

Kim, Sung-Hee. 1906. "The work of party is the duties of the citizen (정당의 사업은 국민의 임무)." *Daehan Hyuphoehoebo*, 1.

Kim, Sung-Hee. 1907. "Liberalism. (자유설)." *Yahroe,* 1.

Kim, Sung-Hee. 1908. "Theory of Independence (독립설)." *Daehan Hyphoehoebo*, 7.

Kim, Yong-Gu. 1997. *The Clash of Worldviews in International Political Science: Eastern propriety and Western public law* (『세계관 충돌의 국제정치학: 동양 예와 서양 공법』). Seoul: Sohwa.

Kim, Yong-Gu. 2008. *International Law* (『만국 공법』). Seoul: Sohwa.

Kim, Young-Myung and Sang Sook Jeon. 2013. "Changes in traditional community consciousness and the shaping of a modern 'national' consciousness: Landmarks in the concept of a nation (전통적 공동체 의식의 변화와 근대 '민족' 인식의 형성: 민족 개념 형성의 계기들)." *Sahoe Yeeron*, 43, 303–329.

Lee, Gak-Jong. 1907. "State science (국가학)." *Sonyunhanbando*, 3.

Lee, Gi-Joon. 1985. *The Introduction of Western Economics in Late Chosun* (『한말 서구 경제학 도입사연구』). Seoul: Iljogak.

Lee, Tae-Jin. 1997. “Historical Insights on the adoption of modern Western political systems (서양 근대 정치제도 수용의 역사적 성찰).” *Jindanhakbo,* 84, 73–133.

Lee, Wan-Jae. 1998. “Early Modern Korean Enlightenment Thought (『한국근대초기개화사상연구』).” Seoul: Hanyang University Press.

Lee, Won-Soon. 1979. “The Western Learning Theory of Silhak (Realist School of Confucianism) Intellectuals during Late Chosun (조선 후기 실학지성의 서양교학론).” *Gyohoesa Yeonghu,* 2, 139–193.

Lee, Won-Soon. 1992. *Treatises on the History of the Chosun Dynasty* (『조선시대사논총』). Seoul: Neutinamu.

Manicas, Peter T. 1987. *A History and Philosophy of the Social Sciences.* Oxford: Basil Blackwell.

Masao, Ichimata. 1973. *Founders of Japanese International Law* (『日本の國際法を築いた人びと』). Gukjaemunjaeshinsuh, 37.

Masao, Maruyama. 1961. *Japanese Thought* (『日本の思想』). Tokyo: Ampa Suhjum.

Matsumoto, Sannosuke. 1969. 『天皇制國家と政治思想. (*The Imperial State and Political Thought*)』. Tokyo: Miraesa.

Moon, Jeung-Sup. 1998. *The Adoption of Western Political Thought in Late Chosun* (『한말의 서양정치사상 수용』). Busan: Kyungsung University Press.

Moon, Seung-Ik. 1979. “Issues in the establishment of Korean political science (한국정치학의 정립문제: 정치이론의 경우).” *Hangukjungchihoebo,* 13, 283-284.

Motoyama, Yukihiko. 1998. *Education Thought of the Meiji State* (『明治國家の教育思想』). Kyoto: Samungak Choolpan.

Muto, Shutaro. 2009. *Modern Japanese Social Science and East Asia* (『近代日本の社會科學と東アジア』). Tokyo: Deungwon Suhjum.

Okita, Yukuzi. 2007. *The Intellectual History of Modern Japanese Education* (『日本近代教育の思想史研究』). Tokyo: Haksoolchoolpanhoe.

Park, Doo-Hwa. 1908. "Editorial: Intangible elements (i.e. sovereignty) in the establishment of a state (논설: 국가성립의 무형요소(즉 통치권))." *Bubjunghakgye,* 1.

Park, Myung-Goo. 2009. *The Nation, the People, and the Citizens* (『국민, 인민, 시민』). Seoul: Sohwa.

Park, Sang-Sup. 2008. *State, Sovereignty* (『국가, 주권』). Seoul: Sohwa.

Research Institute for Korean Church History. 1979. *Selected Readings on the Korean Catholic Church, 11* (『한국 천주교회 논문선집 11』). Seoul: Research Institute for Korean Church History.

Shin, Yong-Ha. 2006. *Research of Independent Community* (『독립협회연구』). Seoul: Iljogak.

Wagner, Peter, Carol Hirschon Weiss, Bjorn Wittrock, and Hellmut Wollmann, eds. 1991. *Social Sciences and Modern States: National Experiences and Theoretical Crossroads*. Cambridge: Cambridge University Press.

Wallerstein, Immanuel. 1994. "History in Search of Science." International Meeting sponsored by the Department of Physics and of History and Geography of the University of Pavia.

Wallerstein, Immanuel. 1994. *Unthinking Social Science: The limits of 19th century paradigms* (『사회과학으로부터의 탈피: 19세기 패러다임의 한계』). Translated by Baek-Yong Sung. Seoul: Changjak-gwa Bipyungsa.

Yamamuro, Shinichi. 1984. *The Era of Legal Bureaucrats: State plans and the journey of knowledge* (『法制官僚の時代 -國の設計と知の歷

程』). Tokyo: Moktaksa.

Yeungnam University National Culture Research Institute. 2000. *An Outline of Korean Cultural Thought 2* (『한국문화사상대계 2』). Gyeongsan: Yeungnam University Press.

CHAPTER 3.

Korea and Early American Anthropology

Robert Oppenheim*

This paper reflects a broader project of writing a history of the American discipline of anthropology's late nineteenth and early twentieth century engagement with Korea, which is explored in more depth in a recently published book.[1] The story I recount here, and more fully in *An Asian Frontier*, is largely untold. In the canonical memory of the American discipline, it is close to an accepted truth that anthropology was dominated by the study of Native Americans until the early 1900s, and that it expanded its global pretensions only slowly until after 1945. And even then, a statement that Korea has not been an area of theoretical importance to American anthropology until relatively re-

* University of Texas at Austin

1 Oppenheim, *An Asian Frontier*. In this article I abstract the arguments of several sections of this larger work.

cently would brook little argument from many practitioners. Meanwhile, intellectual historians of East Asia have devoted attention to the development of Korean folklore studies, Chosŏnhak, and other auto-ethnological practices out of existing domestic and imported intellectual trends from the late nineteenth century onwards, as well as the interest shown Korea by nascent Japanese anthropology from the 1890s, culminating in a great deal of analysis of anthropology as colonial form of knowledge from 1905 or 1910 to 1945. But again, the idea that Korea was something other than a blank space in the world vision of American anthropology in this period has not been greatly explored.

At some level, I do want to say that this picture of a past American discipline uninterested in Korea is simply mistaken—and for some audiences interested in the history of social science knowledge of Korea, this may be sufficient justification for my project. Yet I also aim to use Korea as a standpoint from which to interrogate what might be called, with a degree of heuristic imprecision, the canonical historical account of the American discipline. My larger goal is to work through Korea as secondary but not entirely marginalized area to examine the dialogue between area study and early American anthropology, including the theoretical frameworks and political commitments that it developed over its course.

This also points to the broadest historiographical claim that this project offers. It aims, from the notion of an "Asian frontier" on forward, to be suggestive of the possibility of a "Pacificist" history of American anthropology. My sense of the term invokes the Korean War historian Bruce Cumings in his own turn to American history in *Dominion from Sea to Sea*.[2] It regards Pacificism as a posture in the location of U.S. history as part of world history. This posture regards westward continental expansion and the United States' Pacific involvements beginning in the late eighteenth century, largely oriented toward East Asia, as linked dynamics. I aim to recenter nineteenth and early twentieth century American anthropology, conventionally understood as a science linked to projects of knowing and governing Native American populations on the continental U.S. frontier, within the broader trans-Pacific horizons that a Pacificist frame highlights. Thus, I try to show how Asia (and especially Korea, of course) was articulated with theoretical and ethical turns of American anthropology of the period. Questions of race in relation to aboriginal American populations reached across the Pacific in search of origins; there were more subtle relations of interdependence in narratives of evolution. And the cultural turn, I would argue, found an early comeuppance in Korea that might lead to a reconsideration of the historical valorization of that category. Meanwhile, American anthropology's developing ethical stance in the first half of the twentieth century against racism and to some degree against European imperialisms in conjunction found its own complexities both in the United States' own overseas empire in Hawaii and the Philippines and in different ways in which race (and racism) operated in Korea under Japanese colonial rule.

I. Institutional Development and Collecting Networks

Yet there is a narrow sense in which "Pacificism" is relevant as well. In its first moments as a significant object for American anthropology, at a time when the focus of anthropology was museum collecting, Korea

---

2 Cumings, *Dominion from Sea to Sea*, ix-xv.

was a privileged site on what I call the discipline's "naval frontier." Objects begin to wend their way toward American ethnological museums roughly a half an hour after the May 22, 1882 signing of the first treaty between Chosŏn and the United States, when Commodore Robert Wilson Shufeldt received gifts from his Korean counterparties that, in part, ended up in the Smithsonian two decades later. By 1884, the Smithsonian's U.S. National Museum had two dedicated collectors operating in the peninsula. One, John Baptiste Bernadou, was an actual Navy officer, while the other, Pierre Louis Jouy, was a longer-term Smithsonian employee who had been assigned to a naval survey ship operating in Japanese waters before he diverted himself to Seoul and then Pusan. Behind Bernadou at least was a more substantive conjuncture. The 1882 moment of Korea's "opening" to the U.S. corresponded also with a reorganization of the National Museum that brought it new scale, ambition, and professionalism, and more specifically with a Smithsonian-Navy cooperative program that, from 1881 onwards, brought an annual crop of six young Annapolis graduates to the museum for scientific training in exchange for their services on the Smithsonian's behalf and with the Navy's assistance.[3] So, in short, the museum was gaining new ambition and global reach just as Korea became available. Bernadou was in the second class of the Smithsonian-Navy program, and was destined for laboratory training in chemistry and mineralogy before he volunteered—or was volunteered—to collect in Korea instead; Korea became the first terrestrial target of the program, whence at least some of its late nineteenth century significance.[4]

---

[3] On the National Museum's transition, see Hinsley, *Savages and Scientists*, 74, 94-95; on the Smithsonian-Navy program, see Baird, "Report of Professor Baird…for 1882," 41-42.

Looking at this anthropological collecting from the 1880s through the first decade of the 1900s, it is important to see the complexity of the networks that brought Korean items to U.S. museums and made them ethnologically significant. On the one hand, there are aspects of a conventional story, in which one may find various agents operating in Korea on behalf of a set of U.S. museums, sometimes collecting according to a preordained design, and shipping objects back to the hands of metropolitan curators, who, through the choices of arrangement and labeling, invest them with meaning. So, for instance, there were Bernadou and Jouy working for curators Otis Mason and Walter Hough at the National Museum, with some of Jouy's items also passing to the hands of Edward S. Morse at the Salem Peabody; there was the missionary Eli Barr Landis collecting for the new museum at his alma mater, the University of Pennsylvania; and for a brief period there was C.C. Vinton collecting Korean materials for Franz Boas at the American Museum of Natural History.[5] Even within the purview of this story, there are some interesting considerations. When Bernadou's items arrived at the National Museum, curator Otis Mason wrote, in an 1886 article entitled "Corea by Native Artists" that offers the initial American gloss of Korea's anthropological significance, "we have there," i.e. in Korea, "a human exemplification of the survival of whole genera of industries and customs, while in surrounding regions these have been swept away or transformed."[6] The language of "survivals," ossifications of custom left behind by the general flow of social progress, quoted the great evolutionary theorist of the age,

---

4 Houchins, *An Ethnography of the Hermit Kingdom*, 15, also discusses Bernadou's involvement.

5 On Vinton and Boas, see Kendall, "So Close to the Canon, but…"

6 Mason, "Korea by Native Artists, 115.

E.B. Tylor.[7] But even in Mason's statement there is an ambivalence worth hearing, between a claim of survival-land Korea's universal significance —"human exemplification"—and its solely regional importance— "surrounding regions." And this ambivalence, I would argue, carried over to the decisions, or lack thereof, that seem to have attended the first Korean exhibit at the Smithsonian. By 1889, the National Museum curators had organized their Korean materials into a small exhibit, which is very poorly documented. Korean hats seem to have been an emphasis. But the very decision to exhibit the Korean materials separately, in their own dedicated display, was telling in a museum that otherwise tended to arrange anthropological materials in ostensibly universal developmental sequences—torch to oil lamp to light bulb, for instance—without regard to area or society of origin. It was telling, I would argue, that the National Museum curators did not know exactly how to understand or what to do with Korea or its things.

In other ways, however, it is useful to challenge this conventional understanding of how museums work by pointing to ways in which Korean agencies or dynamics extended into museum space. Interpretation, as I take it, is not a sovereign act that rests solely with curators; interpretation is rather a network or ecological effect. First, there is the curious fact that three of the first Koreans to reside long-term in the United States—Pyŏn Su, Sŏ Chaep'il (aka Philip Jaisohn), and Sŏ Kwangbŏm, all exiles from the failure of the 1884 Kapsin Coup—all worked for shorter or longer periods in the late 1880s at the National Museum as assistants to Mason and Hough. They were young, they were junior, and they were foreign, and what they did there is not well attested either

7 See Tylor, *Primitive Culture*, chapter 3 ("Survivals in Culture").

in Smithsonian records or in the published biographical literature, though one has the occasional glimpse.[8] But it is at least enough to highlight the conceptual overlap between evolutionary American anthropology and the evolutionary assumptions of Korean "Enlightenment faction" thought of the era.

Second, there is the interpretive duel that resulted from Bernadou's collection and the first National Museum exhibit. Horace Allen is well known to Korean history for his variety of roles—missionary, doctor, and diplomat among them—to which we need to add collector and correspondent with Washington anthropology. Allen first went to Korea in 1884, and also became embroiled in the Kapsin Coup events, after which his medical skills saved the life of the gravely injured minister Min Yŏngik. For this service, he seems authentically to have become a close and trusted advisor of King Kojong, and he also received many royal gifts, then and subsequently. In 1887, he returned to the U.S. and to Washington, attached to the Korean Legation as "Foreign Secretary" and mediator, to help represent Chosŏn in the US capital. While there, Allen was called on by Otis Mason to help with the cataloging of Bernadou's Korean collection, to which he readily agreed. But once he started, Allen did not much like what he saw—either Bernadou's objects themselves or Mason's framing of them in terms of the issue of "survivals," Allen felt, made Korea seem primitive. On June 18, 1888, Allen wrote William Elliot Griffis to express his frustration. "The idea that the Koreans are

---

[8] See, for instance, 김원모, "서광범 연구," 253; Houchins, *An Ethnography of the Hermit Kingdom*, 20; Hough, "The Bernadou, Allen, and Jouy Korean Collections," 432. The "Mr. Otis" to whom Channing Liem refers to in his biography of Sŏ Chaep'il is, by process of elimination, almost certainly Otis Mason; see Liem, *The First Korean-American*, 113-17.

barbarians is somewhat sustained by the absurd collection in the National Museum," Allen wrote. "Bernadou couldn't have done worse for the Koreans had he tried."[9]

Allen's response, as a diplomat for Korea, was a countercollection. He sought to inject into the National Museum's Korean collection items of a higher workmanship that might depict Korea to the U.S. public in a more civilized light. Chief among these were the royal gifts that Allen had received, which he deposited with the museum in 1889, attaching their provenance by noting with little superscript daggers the items that in fact possessed royal origins on the list he provided. Nor did the buck stop there. Allen would later record that, when he received his initial round of gifts from the court for saving Min Yŏngik, among the items was a Koryŏ celadon bowl. His first petulant reaction was that it was without value. But then court officials explained to him that it was priceless.[10] So overall, we have a picture of the Korean court pressing items that speak of pinnacles of cultural achievement on one of its champions, and even tutoring his connoisseurship, with Allen in turn pushing items into the National Museum to try to bend American perceptions. And this is otherwise consistent with a growing understanding of Kojong's court's cognizance of the transnational construction of its image and its efforts to intervene, through manipulating photography for instance, in that process.[11]

Third, however, we can point to the efficacies of the peninsular economies in which Koryŏ celadon and other highly-wrought ceramic items,

---

[9] Allen to Griffis June 18, 1888, WEGP R38.

[10] For Allen's account, see Allen, *Copy of a Certified Catalogue*, 4-5.

[11] Kwon, "King Gojong's Portrait." My thanks to Hyung Il Pai for this reference.

so capable of speaking Korean historical refinement (albeit with multiple valences), were entangled. The royal gifting of high-refinement ceramics and the economy of their excavation to feed the demand of Japanese and Western enthusiasts, otherwise known as the robbing of Koryŏ tombs (particularly in the Kaesŏng area), were linked and not separable processes, and Allen, for one, would participate in both. But the prestigious aspect of the competition and hunt for ceramic items in the peninsula could, in and of itself, in a manner reminiscent of the Baudrillardian art auction, pull foreign collectors into the Korean "ceramics game."[12] The result is that we find, on several occasions, American collectors who may have gone to Korea with metropolitan anthropological agendas enticed or diverted into competing for ceramics instead.

II. Evolution and Area Study

Otis Mason's ambivalence in 1886 about the place of Korea in evolutionary theory can be followed to one locus of its resolution almost a decade later. To do so is to consider also the first Korea-focused book in American anthropological history, the 1895 work *Korean Games, with Notes on the Corresponding Games of China and Japan.*[13] *Korean Games* was written by the Philadelphia (later, Brooklyn) anthropologist Stewart Culin, but at a deeper level, not fully visible in published text, it was part of a collaborative project between Culin and his great collabo-

---

12 Baudrillard, *For a Critique*, 112-122.

13 Culin, *Korean Games*. This has recently been translated into Korean by 윤광봉; see Culin, 『한국의 놀이』.

rator Frank Hamilton Cushing, mostly known for his work at Zuni Pueblo in western New Mexico, with help also from Pak Yonggyu, one of the assistants at the Korean exhibit at the 1893 Chicago World's Columbian Exposition. From a conceptual perspective, an examination of their joint project opens onto a contemplation of the conditions and logic of collaboration within evolutionary anthropology conceived in terms of its practice and not simply its conclusions, as it worked to create roles for area study even in the most universalist of intellectual systems.

Stewart Culin began his career as an amateur ethnographer of Philadelphia's Chinese community in the 1880s; he deserves to be remembered as among the first, and first sympathetic, anthropologists of Asian-Americans.[14] At the beginning of the 1890s, he was appointed to a curatorial role at the University of Pennsylvania's new Museum of Archaeology and Paleontology. Along the way, he developed an interest in games of chance, which became a feature of his collecting efforts.[15] He also began to be interested in Korea, which he first saw as a locus of Chinese survivals, adopting one reading of Mason's gloss of the country. Culin's growing reputation eventually gained him a place as an assistant to Frederick Ward Putnam in the anthropology section of the 1893 Fair, in charge of a large exhibit on "Religion, Folklore, and Games." There he met and quickly befriended Cushing. He also began frequenting the Chosŏn exhibit in the Arts and Manufactures building of the Fair.[16]

---

14 I have noted this aspect of Culin's past also in Oppenheim, "Fictional Displacements."

15 See, for instance, Culin, *Chinese Games with Dice.*

16 On the Chosŏn exhibit at the 1893 World's Columbian Exposition, see 이민식, 『근대사의 한 장면: 콜럼비아 세계박람회와 한국』; 김영나, "'박람회'라는 전시공간"; Kane, "Korea in the White City."

In the broader project that would encompass *Korean Games*, Culin and Cushing were engaged in their own friendly argument with E.B. Tylor. Decades earlier, the great evolutionary theorist had set out a question that drove much late nineteenth century anthropological inquiry. "When similar arts, customs, beliefs, or legends are found in several distant regions, among peoples not known to be of the same stock," Tylor had asked in 1865, "how is this similarity to be accounted for?" Tylor offered two possible explanations: "the like working of men's minds under like conditions," and "blood relationship or ... intercourse, direct or indirect, between the races among whom it is found."[17] These two possibilities quickly acquired a shorthand of "independent invention" versus "diffusion," and much American and European anthropological practice of the era revolved around establishing which applied in any given instance. But while the two explanations were formally equally possible, what made evolutionary anthropology special—indeed, what made it evolutionary—was encapsulated in the first of the pair. It was "independent invention" that underwrote the promise of uncovering universal laws of human development, common histories reflective of inner logics of human mind and human experience. Within the framework of the theory, it was the prospect of discovering examples of "independent invention" that might thus provide evidence for the "psychic unity of man," a phrase that became something of a code for the argument as a whole.

Notwithstanding this general thrust of his theory, Tylor himself had to allow for diffusion in some cases, and one of the biggest examples concerned the trans-Pacific history of games. Based on the similarity of both play and name between the southern Asian game *pachisi*

[17] Tylor, *Researches into the Early History of Mankind*, 5.

(subsequently copyrighted and sold in the United States as Parcheesi) and the Mesoamerican game *patolli*, Tylor had argued in an 1879 article that this must be a case of direct transmission, via some pathway long lost to history, from the Old World to the New—and of course he assumed that the diffusion had taken place in that direction.[18] Cushing and Culin sought, in what Cushing at least imagined as a chivalric duel with the master himself, to disprove Tylor on games in favor of the more general "independent invention" impetus of Tylorian theory. More specifically, they sought to argue that there had been parallel, independent development of games of chance ultimately from divination using arrows in both eastern Asia and aboriginal America, and therefore that the divination-games developmental sequence represented an immanent unfolding of the human psyche and thus a universal of human evolution. As they analyzed it, the arrow, hurled or shot from a bow, had begun as an agent of fate itself, of death or life, for its target. From there, flipped or thrown onto a sectioned board, it had become a predictor of fate, a tool of divination, and from there the development from the arrow of sticks, then dice, then playing cards represented steps of progressive abstraction. Throughout their correspondence leading up to *Korean Games*, Culin and Cushing tried to convince each other of the existence of this sequence on both sides of the Pacific, with Culin working the Asian side and Cushing the American, and occasionally also of the absence of its intermediate elements along the most likely path of direct transmission, the Bering Strait corridor, in order to rule out an alternative diffusionist explanation.

So for Culin and Cushing, it was the second sequence, an American

[18] Tylor, "On the Game of Patolli."

sequence added to an Asian or an Asian sequence added to an American, that created the possibility of arguing that the sequence itself was a human universal. If we view it "in action," in terms of the internal logic of its verificational practice, we can see an important role for area difference in the making of this universalist evolutionary argument.[19] But just as important is a black boxing effect in which, once a sequence was ostensibly demonstrated as independently copresent and thus universal, its antecedent history of area comparison could be deleted. And this dynamic is key to another aspect of the Culin-Cushing project, namely, that it was an argument for an area-focused claim. Cushing and Culin were and were surrounded by anthropologists who were self-declared "Americanists," who sought to argue the self-sufficiency of American studies as equally revealing of human history as such as any other culture history. This was a position against the Old World philologists and proponents of various theories of cultural diffusion from Old World to New (concerning, for instance, the Mayan pyramids and a host of other civilizational achievements) who, in essence, argued that everything interesting in the history of humanity had happened in the Old World, that America (and by extension American studies) was and could only be derivative. Tylor's argument about *pachisi* and *patolli* had touched a very raw nerve. Hence a central irony: *Korean Games* was the first Korea book in American anthropology, but it spoke for America itself. It was part of a declaration of independence, for the possibility of America representing the universal, and thus for the logical admissibility of ignoring Asia entirely in the future.

To write this, however, is to describe an "as if" version of their proj-

---

[19] See Latour, *Science in Action*, for the sense of this present argument.

ect, a version most present in Culin and Cushing's correspondence rather than actual publications. *Korean Games* only partially came together according to the plan that is evident in unpublished documents, and as a result the larger argument partially fell apart. First, together. Why was the book's focus on Korea, and why was it entitled, in particular, *Korean Games*? It was *Korean Games* because a key moment in the process of Culin and Cushing convincing themselves of their own argument was Culin's discovery of the Korean game *yut* (윷), as demonstrated by Pak Yonggyu, at the Chosŏn exhibit of the 1893 World's Fair. According to Cushing, *yut* closely paralleled a Zuni game, and the sticks that are thrown in its play, hemispherical in cross-section, amounted to a "missing link" in the Asian sequence between arrows and more abstracted randomizers such as dice, dominos, and cards. *Yut* was the survival that mattered in Korea viewed (à la Mason) as a "land of survivals." Then, apart. The argument for independent invention was not clearly articulated in the published version of *Korean Games*. Cushing was intuitively brilliant and the stronger theorist of the two, and during his correspondence with Culin during 1894-95 it was supposed that Cushing would write a theoretical "commentary" to be published in *Korean Games* that would set Culin's mostly descriptive discussion of individual games in the context of their larger joint theory. But part of the package of Cushing's quicksilver personality was that he was a somewhat unreliable, and he suffered from physical ill health and melancholia to boot. As a result the "commentary" anticipated until the eve of publication never happened. Thus the clearest argument in *Korean Games* for their thesis of independent invention is here on the title page, in the four-character Sino-Korean phrase sahaeilga (四海一家), "four seas one family," an invocation (based on Culin's use of it in other documents) of Tylor's quotation of an Italian proverb, "tutto il mondo è paese," "all the world is one country," which Tylor used as a slogan for the argument for the "psychic unity of man."[20] One can perhaps imagine how well Anglophone reviewers and the U.S. reading public picked up on these broader implications—most reviews, at least by those not already in the know, missed them entirely. In a sense, finally, Culin fell apart too. Two years after Cushing died in 1900, Culin published a lecture, "America the Cradle of Asia," that reviewed all the evidence that the pair had used to argue for independent invention. Now, however, Culin argued that this same evidence in fact pointed to a history of diffusion, but diffusion from the New World to the Old, rather than the much more commonly assumed other way around.[21] This was a hypertrophy of Culin's Americanism, which I argue was already lurking in *Korean Games*, but one that extracted it from the logic of his joint theory with Cushing. What had been a counterargument to diffusionism had become simply a counter-diffusionism.

III. Troubling (Anti-)Imperial Anthropologies

Ethnology, folklore, and physical anthropology conducted by Japanese scholars during the colonial period have been the focus of much critical attention from historians.[22] Korean folklore studies undertaken during

---

20 Tylor, *Primitive Culture*, 6.

21 Culin, "American the Cradle of Asia." Lyman, *Color, Culture, Civilization*, 218-38, also makes much of this development, while reading it somewhat differently than I do.

22 See for example 최석영, 『일제하 무속론과 식민지 권력』; 전경수, 『한국인류학 백년』, 46-51; Atkins, *Primitive Selves*, 52-101; Pai, *Constructing "Korean" Origins*; Walraven,

the same era have often been seen to have set the foundation of cultural studies of Korea in the post-1945 period.[23] Yet one may finally consider American anthropology engaged with Korea during the years of Japanese colonial rule. Here my concern is with two figures, Frederick Starr and Aleš Hrdlička, who had controversial but otherwise quite different careers. Starr was the first, somewhat unruly anthropologist at the University of Chicago, and an ethnographer or at least an inveterate traveler. He made six research trips to Korea between 1911 and 1930 (and far more to Japan over the roughly the same span of time), bracketing his formal retirement from the university in 1923. Hrdlička was the Bohemian-American curator of physical anthropology at the Smithsonian's National Museum, an expert on anthropometry and a somewhat cranky elder statesman in the field. He went to Korea only once, in the 1920 wake of the March First uprisings, but Korea occupied one pole of his thinking right up to his death in 1943. Here, I consider Starr and Hrdlička in constellation, because in constellation they show how an engagement with Korea could shift the implications of the Boasian settlement within American anthropology, a turn in the history of the American discipline that is still often considered formative of its tendencies and influence in the second half of the twentieth century.[24] What do I mean by this term, "Boasian settlement"? From roughly the turn of the century through the 1940s, but perhaps gathering steam from the 1910s, Franz Boas and his students precipitated a fundamental shift in the conceptual architecture, practice, and ethics of American anthropology that still underlies

---

"The Natives Next Door."

[23] E.g., Janelli, "The Origins of Korean Folklore Scholarship."

[24] On the importance of this development, see variously Stocking, *Race, Culture, and Evolution*; Bunzl, "Franz Boas"; Darnell, *And along Came Boas*.

much of what it has become. First, they established that culture, language, and race vary independently. Mental characteristics, or the propensity to speak certain languages, do not derive from physical traits. Second, and here I follow in particular Michel-Rolph Trouillot, they engaged in an internal redistribution of the characteristics of culture and race as categories.[25] Culture became a way of talking about human difference that insisted on the historicity of difference; it denied ontology. Race, which in previous treatments had sometimes included capacities for Lamarckian change that might surprise us today, was recast as a claim of the ontological somatic. Third, this redefinition of the architecture of race as a concept was a step toward its demolition, which they also initiated. The physical traits that ostensibly cluster in human races or types themselves have independent clinal distributions, they argued; race (or type) is thus an artificial average, an epiphenomenon. Moreover, some physical characteristics, such as height, vary greatly in response to environmental determinants, such as nutrition.[26] It is from this moment that "race" gains scare-quotes in much anthropological writing, comes to be treated (if at all) as a social construct rather than an adequate way of considering physical difference.[27] Fourth and finally, this elevation of culture and historicity over race and ontology was also a liberal-progressive scientific response to racial discrimination in the United States and toward potential immigrants, to European imperialisms grounded in

---

[25] Trouillot, "Adieu, Culture."

[26] This was famously argued by Boas in a 1912 article; see Boas, "Changes in the Bodily Form of Descendants of Immigrants."

[27] For the wartime demolition of the race concept in the hands of students and allies of Boas, see Benedict, *Race: Science and Politics*; and Montagu, *Man's Most Dangerous Myth*.

colonial racism, and eventually to Nazism. As outlined here, this way of thinking partially inaugurated by the Boasians may well be familiar; it remains basic to global liberal sensibilities today.

But did this Boasian settlement represent a universal scientific politics, even in its historical moment? Many anthropologists, after the practical turn and in the face of multiple contemporary discourses on "culture," are no longer content to use the term as an unproblematic analytic category.[28] But many of these same anthropologists, and dominant voices in disciplinary memory, would argue that "culture" gave anthropology important critical leverage against the several evils of the world just mentioned at the moment of its initial articulation. Now let me turn to Starr in colonial Korea.[29] Over the course of his visits Starr gained in sympathy for the situation of Koreans even as he shifted from an interest in Korean racial history and physical deformity to planning a book called *Korean Culture*. Yet the story of his shift cannot be told in the usual way of disciplinary historiography, namely, that he simply followed conceptual developments in the discipline and began to apply them in his own work. He was aware of these developments, but the division of inside and outside is not so clear: Starr's "culture" was simultaneously being formatted by the prevalent Taishō discourse on culture and by the discourse on culture in colonial Korea, encapsulated in the post-1919 governmental policy turn toward "cultural rule" and by the Korean "cultural movement," what Michael Robinson described as "cultural nationalism."[30]

---

[28] On the practical turn in anthropology, see Ortner, "Theory in Anthropology since the Sixties"; for one perception of the history and problems of the category of culture, see again Trouillot, "Adieu, Culture."

[29] I leave out here arguments I present elsewhere against the usual biographical reading of Starr, though it should be known that these exist.

Starr's best Korean associates and intellectual interlocutors were cultural movement intellectuals Yi Nŭnghwa and Ch'oe Namsŏn. And he reproduced the meliorism and the deferral of cultural nationalist politics. By the end of his time in Korea, Starr was giving talks in which he advised Koreans to "know thyself," to study their history and their culture, but not to strive for independence in anything but the ever-receding long-term future. What conclusions can be drawn from this arc? First, Starr's Korean culture is the product of a mutual tuning between the American anthropological category and the already present discourse on culture in the colonial setting of the 1920s; there was not a moment, even then, when the anthropological analytic had temporal or logical precedence. And thus, second, if we see American anthropology's culture as existing within a larger topology of the term, at least in colonial Korea it failed to provide any leverage against imperialism. American anthropology's culture arrived in Korea pre-limited in its political potential. Starr, personally, had a wide-ranging politics that was often deeply anti-imperialist; he was disbelieving of the claims of a *mission civilisatrice* offered by many imperial powers. But out of his own internal logic he made exceptions for Japan in Korea and Belgium in the Congo. His Korean use of "culture" as an anti-anti-imperialist category was part and parcel of that exception.

Hrdlička, then, was in some respects Starr's antithesis. He was the strongest advocate that Korean independence had in American anthropology, or at least the strongest I have found. And he did so using racialist categories, rejecting the Boasian settlement of race and culture and con-

---

30 See, for example, Robinson, *Cultural Nationalism in Colonial Korea*; Sand, "The Cultured Life as Contested Space."

tinuing to accept the covariation of physical and mental traits, and taking many positions that were unquestionably racist—Hrdlicka was, in particular, a strong white supremacist who in 1922 testified to Congress against Japanese immigration.[31] The conceptual basis of his argument for Korean independence was rooted in his particular construction of the category of type and the supposed historical process of typogeny. While much racialist anthropology was basically concerned with questions of descent, of the derivation of human populations ultimately from the great, color-coded racial "stems," typogeny was, for Hrdlicka, a second order historical process. It authorized the question, looking at nation-sized units, of whether the "mixed stock" from which nations were invariably derived had re-integrated to form a coherent national type. "Type" was thus a live, empirical, *a posteriori* question for Hrdlicka, which allowed him to argue that, anthropologically speaking, a given nation did or did not exist—whatever its members might think.

We can begin to see what Hrdlička did with this category in this 1942 quotation of him in the Hawai`i Korean nationalist press.

> Dr. Aleš Hrdlička of the Smithsonian Institution and one of the foremost anthropologists of the world in a recent interview . . . stated "the Japanese is the world's prime hybrid—a mixture of Eskimo, Mongol, Chinese, Korean, Malay, Negrito, Ainu, white man and a long extinct new stone age race."
>
> Dr. Hrdlička referred to the Koreans as a "unique race," and "are nearer white men than any other people of eastern Asia, have many white physical

[31] See United States House of Representatives, *Nonassimilability of Japanese in Hawaii and the United States*.

characteristics and seem to 'think like white men' more than either Chinese or Japanese."[32]

Our eyes may be drawn to his claim of the "whiteness" of Koreans. But the more important claim and argument for Korean independence within Hrdlička's overall thought was the contention that the Japanese remained hybrid, mixed, non-integrated, an unrealized type, while Koreans were "unique," possessed strong definition, and represented successful typogeny. In the larger scheme of his politics, Koreans would line up with Hrdlička's own natal Czechs as ennobled, typologically-integrated small nations struggling against non-integrated imperial forces, whether imperial Japan, Austria-Hungary before 1918, or imperialist Nazi Germany after 1938.

All this may be of mostly historical relevance, although the point that racialism remained present in global anthropologies well after its supposed Boasian sell-by date is well worth underscoring.[33] His position on Korea aside, Hrdlička's racialism is, to put it mildly, unappealing. But what is of more than passing interest in considering Hrdlička is less his answer than the question he was addressing. Among American anthropologists of the interwar era, Hrdlička may have been uniquely cognizant and critical of a kind of political deployment of the category of "race" that escaped the Boasian ken, what may be heuristically thought of as a "second problematic of racism," and this was on display for him most prominently in the anthropological politics of Japanese colonial rule in

32 *Korean National Herald—Pacific Weekly*, February 25, 1942.

33 Hoi-eun Kim emphasizes this point in a forthcoming article; see Kim, "Re-authenticating Race."

Korea.[34] Hrdlička made a trip to northeast Asia in 1920, shortly after the colonial state's forcible suppression of countrywide protests that followed the March 1, 1919 Korean Declaration of Independence. In his notes and unpublished memoir, he revealed clear sympathy for Koreans who had been flogged to death, hanged, or imprisoned for (as he put it) "patriotism." He also encountered for the first time a legitimating anthropological claim sometimes espoused by Japanese officials and sympathetic intellectuals. Under the rubric of *Nissen dōsoron*, "the theory of common Japanese and Korean [racial] origins," many such intellectuals had naturalized and justified the Japanese takeover of the peninsula as more or less a family reunion, a joining of peoples already fundamentally related. Later, from the late 1930s, *Nissen dōsoron* helped underwrite a more radically assimilationist policy of making Koreans Japanese by mandating the use of Japanese names and Japanese language, demanding participation in state Shintō ceremonies, and strongly encouraging young Korean men to join the military and fight and die for the Emperor. Now of course there was also simultaneously a great deal of discrimination against Koreans, but it was this racialist claim of fundamental identity between Koreans and Japanese to political effect, this "racism of sameness," that Hrdlička picked up on. And from virtually the moment of his return from Asia in 1920, perhaps even before, Hrdlička was contesting the racism of sameness in Japanese Korea on anthropological grounds. In 1920's "The Anthropological Problems of the Far East," for example, he wrote that "the Japanese in general, for political reasons, are rather anxious to convince the Koreans, as well as others, that the

---

34 Worth noting in connection is the virtual absence of Korea—or thus considerations of the politics of race in the Japanese empire—in Ruth Benedict's famous *The Chrysanthemum and the Sword.*

Koreans are the same as themselves, but the scientific observer sees readily substantial differences, at least as large as those between the Koreans and Chinese."[35] His depiction of Koreans as a successfully integrated type, and of Japanese as irredeemably hybrid, began in the same moment.

The most important point is thus that Hrdlička perceived the politically-enunciated assimilationist claim of identity as itself a racism, a possibility that largely escaped Boas and his students. And this failure of American anthropology beyond Hrdlička, at the moment of the Boasian settlement and its initial articulation of an antiracialist critique, to overcome the elision of this critique with simple opposition to a racism of difference (as necessary, of course, as that opposition is) continues to bedevil the discipline today. Thus the politics of colonial Korea trouble the Boasian settlement. "Culture" had no answer to Japanese imperialism. Racialism did, but more importantly, that it took racialism to have an answer shows us blind spots in the Boasian critique of race.

IV. Conclusion

In this paper, I have sought to review the conceptual exchange and interaction patterns of American anthropology and Korea before 1945, a project that I pursue much more fully in *An Asian Frontier*. At the end of this project, the question arises: what sort of conclusions is it possible to draw about the implications and aftereffects of these sixty years of interaction? Such conclusions can only be fairly modest. I have not sought to identify some positive intellectual legacy or theoretical tendency that

[35] Hrdlička, "The Anthropological Problems of the Far East," 570.

persisted into anthropology after 1945, no "gatekeeping concepts" that have driven the anthropology of Korea since.[36] There is no straight, determinative line from past to present, and certainly there is no counterhero or champion from the mists of time whom I would wish to revive and set loose upon the discipline. Moreover, the interactions between Koreans and American scholars that I document were often asymmetrical in a variety of ways. Starr, for instance, was deeply influenced by Ch'oe Namsŏn and especially Yi Nŭnghwa, whom he viewed as a cosmopolitan *par excellence*,[37] but I have searched in vain for any record that Ch'oe or Yi were reciprocally influenced by Starr. What this history does offer, however, is perhaps most signaled by the character of Korea's relation to the "Boasian settlement" with which I concluded. Korea was by no means ignored in American anthropological history, but it was repeatedly "off-center" with conceptual formations defining of the discipline, a bad fit, and perhaps to this history clings a rather more relational legacy of displacement itself. One step further, I aim to suggest the value of a different and more transnational sort of genealogy than national intellectual histories, or "Korean studies" as usually conceived of outside of Korea, usually perform. It would be one thing to do a genealogy of Korean thought on race and culture, or a genealogy of metropolitan understandings of these concepts in American anthropology, for example—these are familiar forms of scholarship. But an alternative is to perform a genealogy not of a local Korean or American set of ideas but of a fractured transnational conversation to which both were a party from its inception, co-present but displaced from each other, out of whack,

36 On "gatekeeping concepts," see Appadurai, "Theory in Anthropology," 357.

37 See Starr, *Korean Buddhism*, 37.

generating meaning out of resonance and interference. This is an aspect of what I have attempted to do in this project.

■ REFERENCES

Archival Sources:

WEGP: William Elliot Griffis Papers, Special Collections and University Archives, Rutgers University Libraries, New Brunswick, NJ. Microfilm publication as *Japan Through Western Eyes: Manuscript Records of Traders, Travellers, Missionaries & Diplomats, 1853-1941*, parts 2-5, Adam Matthew, 2000.

Published Sources:

Allen, Allen, Horace N. *Copy of a Certified Catalogue of a Collection of Ancient Korean Pottery*. Nak Tong: The Seoul Press, 1901.

Appadurai, Arjun. "Theory in Anthropology: Center and Periphery." *Comparative Studies in Society and History* 28, no. 2 (April 1986): 356-361.

Atkins, E. Taylor. *Primitive Selves: Koreana in the Japanese Colonial Gaze*, 1910-1945. Berkeley: University of California Press, 2010.

Baird, Spencer F. "Report of Professor Baird, Secretary of the Smithsonian Institution, for 1882." In *Annual Report of the Board of Regents of the Smithsonian Institution, Showing the Operation, Condition, and Expenditures of the Institution for the Year 1882*, 1-56. Washington: Government Printing Office, 1884.

Baudrillard, Jean. *For a Critique of the Political Economy of the Sign.* Translated by Charles Levin. St. Louis: Telos Press, 1981.

Benedict, Ruth. *The Chrysanthemum and the Sword: Patterns of Japanese Culture.* Boston: Houghton Mifflin, 1946.

_______. *Race: Science and Politics.* New York: Modern Age Books, 1940.

Boas, Franz. "Changes in the Bodily Form of Descendants of Immigrants." *American Anthropologist* 14, no. 3 (July-September 1912): 530-562.

Bunzl, Matti. "Franz Boas and the Humboldtian Tradtion: From *Volksgeist* and *Nationalcharakter* to an Anthropological Concept of Culture." In Volksgeist *as Method and Ethic: Essays on Boasian Ethnography and the German Anthropological Tradition*, edited by George W. Stocking, Jr., 17-78. Madison: University of Wisconsin, 1996.

Culin, Stewart. "America the Cradle of Asia." *Harper's Monthly* 106 (May 1903): 534-40.

_______. *Chinese Games with Dice.* Philadelphia: Oriental Club of Philadelphia, 1889.

_______. *Korean Games, With Notes on the Corresponding Games of China and Japan.* Philadelphia: University of Pennsylvania, 1895.

Cumings, Bruce. *Dominion from Sea to Sea: Pacific Ascendancy and American Power.* New Haven: Yale University Press, 2009.

Darnell, Regna. *And Along Came Boas: Continuity and Revolution in Americanist Anthropology.* Amsterdam: John Benjamins, 1998.

Hinsley, Curtis. *Savages and Scientists: The Smithsonian Institution and the Development of American Anthropology, 1846-1910.* Washington DC: Smithsonian Institution Press, 1981.

Houchins, Chang-su Cho. *An Ethnography of the Hermit Kingdom: The J.B. Bernadou Korean Collection 1884-1885.* Washington: Smithsonian

Institution, 2004.

Hough, Walter. “The Bernadou, Allen, and Jouy Korean Collections in the U.S. National Museum.” In *Annual Report of the Board of Regents of the Smithsonian Institution, Showing the Operation, Condition, and Expenditures of the Institution for the Year Ending June 30, 1891. Report of the U.S. National Museum*, 429-88. Washington: Government Printing Office, 1892.

Hrdlička, Aleš. “The Anthropological Problems of the Far East.” *Science* 52, no. 1355 (December 1920): 567-74.

Janelli, Roger L. “The Origins of Korean Folklore Scholarship.” *The Journal of American Folklore* 99, no. 391 (January-March 1986): 24-49.

Kane, Daniel. “Korea in the White City: Korean Participation in the World’s Colombian Exposition of 1893.” *Transactions of the Korea Branch of the Royal Asiatic Society* 77 (2002): 1-57.

Kendall, Laurel. “So Close to the Canon, but...of Franz Boas, C.C. Vinton, and Some Korean Things.” *Journal of Korean Studies*, forthcoming.

Kim, Hoi-eun. “Re-authenticating Race: Rha Saejin and the Recycling of Colonial Physical Anthropology in Post-Colonial Korea.” *Journal of Korean Studies*, forthcoming.

Kwon Heangga. “King Gojong’s Portrait and the Advent of Photography in Korea.” Yun Heejin, trans. *Journal of Korean Art and Archaeology* 5 (2011): 58-69.

Latour, Bruno. *Science in Action: How to Follow Scientists and Engineers through Society*. Cambridge: Harvard University Press, 1987.

Liem, Channing. *The First Korean-American—A Forgotten Hero: Philip Jaisohn*. Philadelphia: The Philip Jaisohn Memorial Foundation, 1984.

Lyman, Stanford M. *Color, Culture, Civilization: Race and Minority Issues in American Society*. Urbana: University of Illinois Press, 1994.

Mason, Otis Tufton. "Corea by Native Artists." *Science* (n.s.) 8, no. 183 (August 1886): 115-18.

Montagu, M.F. Ashley. *Man's Most Dangerous Myth: The Fallacy of Race*. New York: Columbia University Press, 1942.

Oppenheim, Robert. *An Asian Frontier: American Anthropology and Korea, 1882-1945*. Lincoln: University of Nebraska Press, 2016.

_______. "Fictional Displacements: Stewart Culin's Heaven and Earth." *Anthropology and Humanism* 36, no. 2 (December 2011): 164-77.

Ortner, Sherry B. "Theory in Anthropology since the Sixties." *Comparative Studies in Society and History* 26, no. 1 (January 1984): 126-66.

Pai, Hyung Il. *Constructing "Korean" Origins: A Critical Review of Archaeology, Historiography, and Racial Myth in Korean State-Formation Theories*. Cambridge: Harvard University Asia Center, 2000.

Robinson, Michael Edson. *Cultural Nationalism in Colonial Korea, 1920-1925*. Seattle: University of Washington Press, 1988.

Sand, Jordan. "The Cultured Life as Contested Space: Dwelling and Discourse in the 1920s." In *Being Modern in Japan: Culture and Society from the 1910s to the 1930s*, edited by Elise K. Tipton and John Clark, 99-118. Honolulu: University of Hawai'i Press, 2000.

Starr, Frederick. *Korean Buddhism: History—Condition—Art*. Boston: Marshall Jones, 1918.

Stocking, George W., Jr. *Race, Culture, and Evolution: Essays in the History of Anthropology*. New York: Free Press, 1968.

Trouillot, Michel-Rolph. "Adieu, Culture: A New Duty Arises." *In*

Anthropology beyond Culture, edited by Richard G. Fox and Barbara J. King, 37–60. Oxford: Berg, 2002.

Tylor, Edward Burnett. *Researches into the Early History of Mankind and the Development of Civilization*. Second edition. London: John Murray, 1870.

_______. "On the Game of Patolli in Ancient Mexico, and Its Probably Asiatic Origin." *The Journal of the Anthropological Institute of Great Britain and Ireland* 8 (1879): 116-31.

_______. *Primitive Culture: Researches into the Development of Mythology, Philosophy, Religion, Language, Art and Custom*. Third American Edition. New York: Henry Holt and Company, 1889.

United States House of Representatives. *Nonassimilability of Japanese in Hawaii and the United States*. Hearings before the Committee on the Territories, House of Representatives, Sixty-seventh Congress, second session, July 17. Washington, DC: Government Printing Office, 1922.

Walraven, Boudewijn. "The Natives Next-Door: Ethnology in Colonial Korea." In *Anthropology and Colonialism in Asia and Oceania*, edited by Jan van Bremen and Akitoshi Shimizu, 219-44. Richmond, Surrey: Taylor & Francis, 1999.

김영나. "'박람회' 라는 전시공간: 1893년 시카고 만국 박람회와 조선관 전시." 『서양 미술사 학회 논문집』. 13(2000): 75-106.

김원모. "서광범 연구 (1859-1897)." 『동양학』. 15 (1984): 239-80.

이민식. 『근대사의 한 장면: 콜럼비아 세계박람회와 한국』. 서울: 백산자료원, 2006.

전경수. 『한국인류학 백년』. 서울: 일지사, 1999.

최석영. 『일제하 무속론과 식민지 권력』. 서울: 서경문화사, 1999.

스튜어트 컬린. 『한국의 놀이: 유사한 중국 – 일본의 놀이와 비교하여』. 윤광봉 역. 서울: 열화당, 2003.

CHAPTER 4.

Shinzo Koizumi(1888-1966): A Japanese Economist's Encounter with the West*

Yukihiro Ikeda**

I. A Brief Overview of the Life of Shinzo Koizumi[1]

Shinzo Koizumi was born in Tokyo in 1888. The son of Nobukichi Koizumi, an influential personality at Keio Gijuku during the Meiji Era, Koizumi studied economics at Keio

* An earlier version of this paper was read at the 2005 HETSA meeting at Macquarie University, Sydney. I would like to thank the participants and two anonymous referees for their comments. The Japanese version of the paper was published in the following form: Yukihiro Ikeda, 'Shinzo Koizumi (1886-1966): A Japanese Economist's Encounter with the West' (in Japanese), *Keio Business Review* 48(5), December, 2005. My thanks also go to the Society of Business and Commerce, Keio University, for kind permission to reproduce the paper in English. Throughout this paper Japanese names are given in the Western order, that is, first name and then surname. For a good introduction to the Japanese history of economic thought in general, I would suggest the following literature for English readers: Sugihara and Tanaka (1998); Sugiyama and Mizuta (1988); Sugiyama (1994). And the paper was published in *History of Economics Review*, 44 (Summer, 2006).

** Department of Economics, Keio University, Mita 2-15-45, Minato-ku 108-8345, Tokyo, Japan. Email: ikeda@econ.keio.ac.jp.

1 For a biographical description of Koizumi, see Koizumi (1966).

University, and was hired by the university as a junior faculty member in April 1910. An important mentor of Koizumi's was Tokuzo Fukuda[2], an economist who contributed much to the introduction of Western economics in Japan. From September 1912 to March 1916, Koizumi lived abroad in Britain, Germany, and France. Upon returning to Japan, he was immediately named a full professor. Koizumi played an important role not only as a scholar but also in the administration of Keio University: he served as the president of the university from 1933 to 1947, a difficult time indeed for Keio. After the war, Koizumi continued to write prolifically, emerging as one of the most famous conservative voices in postwar Japan. Koizumi is also well known for having served as a tutor of the Japanese Crown Prince (now Emperor) beginning in 1949. Koizumi died in 1966.

A bird's-eye view of Koizumi's position in the history of Japanese politico-economic thought will be helpful in approaching my main topic, Koizumi's years abroad. First, Koizumi's debates with Japanese Marxists on the plausibility of Marx's economic reasoning are widely remembered. Among the many Marxists with whom he debated were Hajime Kawakami and Tamizo Kushida. Even from a Marxist perspective, these debates can certainly be understood to have contributed to deepening the understanding of Marxist thought in Japan. Koizumi's 'Marx, Fifty Years After His Death' (1933) and 'Criticism of Communism: Common Sense' (1949), moreover, were widely read among Japanese conservatives who were critical of Marxism.

Secondly, Koizumi contributed greatly to the diffusion of both classi-

---

[2] For Fukuda as well as his relationship with the German Historical School, see Nishizawa (2001).

cal and neoclassical economics in Japan. His Japanese translation of William Stanley Jevons's *Theory of Political Economy* (1913), with an introduction by Fukuda, made Koizumi's name in the academic world. Koizumi later translated David Ricardo's *Principles of Political Economy and Taxation* (1928), a *magnum opus* of the English Classical School. How could the translator of Jevons's principal work also undertake the translation of Ricardo, Jevons's *bête noire*? This is an intriguing question that merits extended discussion.

In this essay, however, I focus upon Koizumi's encounter with Western culture as a young Japanese economist, considering in particular Koizumi's time abroad. In sections 2 and 3, I deal with his stays in England and Germany, respectively. In the last section I offer a short epilogue and concluding remarks.

Almost all of Koizumi's diary entries to which I shall refer are drawn from *A Diary of Young Shinzo Koizumi from 1911 to 1914*: Tokyo, London, and Berlin, Keio University Press, 2001. (Hereafter *A Diary of Young Shinzo Koizumi*.) The newly published diary represents an important resource on Koizumi from which much can be learned concerning not only his studies and the development of his economic thought, but also the state of British and German economics shortly before World War I.

II. England

1. Lectures at LSE

After a long sea journey via Shanghai, Hong Kong, Singapore, Suez and Marseilles, Koizumi arrived in London on 7 November 1912. On

9 January 1913 he paid his first visit to the London School of Economics to pay his tuition fees. As he describes it:

> In the afternoon went to LSE to pay tuition fees. I want to visit Cannan's 'History of Economic Thought' (Advanced Level), but one has to get permission from Prof Cannan to attend this lecture. I am going to see him on this coming Tuesday. The same applies to Webb's seminar. Paid 12 shilling 6 pence for Foxwell's banking and currency. In the British Museum, took a look at Cannan's new book, *Economic Outlook*. In the introduction there is an autobiographical essay. A little bit affected but interesting. There is a paper titled 'Ricardo in the Parliament. It looks interesting, but did not have time to read it. (Koizumi 1911-14 [2001], p. 317)

At the time of Koizumi's visit to England, Cannan, in his fifties, was a dominant force at LSE and his name turns up often in Koizumi's diary. As this passage shows, Koizumi was interested in Cannan's newly published book, *Economic Outlook*.

The first entry describing lectures Koizumi attended at LSE is dated 14 January 1913. Koizumi wrote:

> For the first time I attended lectures by Cannan and Foxwell at LSE. The buildings of the School are very dirty. And there were only a few students. Cannan's lecture was based on his *History of the Theories of Production and Distribution*. He spoke very poorly. His speech was drawn out by his 'ah's', which made the lecture unpleasant. He looks

very much like Edward VII. I endured much pain listening to his one- hour lecture. I thought of getting permission to take part in Cannan's special class, but that would be a discussion, not a lecture. He told me that the lecture would be better, so I gave up on attending the special class. There are still fewer students in Foxwell's class on banking and currency. Foxwell has a very scholarly face. I looked at his face, thinking that he certainly photographs well. The lecture was about the history of English currency. He made comments on the government's policy concerning the value of the guinea. (*Ibid.*, p. 318)

The full title of the book by Cannan to which Koizumi refers in this entry is *History of the Theories of Production and Distribution in English Political Economy from 1776 to 1848* (1893). Obviously, Koizumi was not impressed with Cannan's lecturing style. That Cannan was not always a good speaker is confirmed by the following description by another of Cannan's pupils, Lionel Robbins, also a major figure in the history of LSE:

> Certainly he was not a good lecturer, at any rate in the ordinary sense of the term. He could deliver a very lucid and popular lecture when he set himself to do so, as his presidential addresses to the RES have demonstrated. But his normal lectures on Principles were not of this quality. It was not always possible to hear him. His delivery was never fluent and he had a habit of talking into his beard which made parts, and often the most important parts, of his lecture almost inaudible unless you were sitting in the first two rows. Moreover, they were not arranged with a view to the convenience of beginners. (Robbins 1935 [1997], p. 327)

Lionel Robbins's impression of Cannan closely accords with the entry in Koizumi's diary cited above. Nevertheless, on the day after making this entry, Koizumi stayed home to read the representative work of

Cannan's to which the entry referred. Koizumi noted: 'Stayed at home. Read Cannan, Theories of Production and Distribution; and Humphrey, History of Labour Representation' (Koizumi 1911-14 [2001], p. 320). The following description of a conversation with Foxwell deserves to be quoted in full:

> After lecture, put a question to Foxwell. Confirmed my impression that he is rich. After giving a satisfactory answer to my question concerning the introduction to the *Right to the Whole Produce of Labour*, he said, 'The book is out of print and very expensive. I know there is a copy in a bookshop close to the British Museum. But I suppose it costs about 17 shillings. One has to go to several shops to find the cheapest copy'. (In answer to my asking if he meant the Museum Bookshop) 'No, not that one. It's quite expensive there. The owner, a Polish Jew, is very greedy. I had a terrible experience. I can't recommend that shop'. Etc., etc. And, 'If you would like to buy a copy, I can suggest a bookshop in Cambridge. And if you want to buy German books, I would suggest Müller in Grape Street. He is himself a good scholar with excellent publications'. Foxwell is quite different from Cannan. Cannan is blunt, and sour-faced. Foxwell is much more accomplished than Cannan in the academic world. For Cannan, the search for used books is of vital importance; but Foxwell may be better at this as well. The introduction to the *Right to the Whole Produce of Labour* shows this quite clearly. (Koizumi 1911-14 [2001], pp. 339-40)

The *Right to the Whole Produce of Labour* by Anton Menger, younger brother of the famous economist, was one of Koizumi's favourite books. The original German edition appeared as early as 1886; its English translation was published in 1899, with a well-known introduction by Foxwell.

On 4 December 1912, Koizumi borrowed a copy of the English translation from a Japanese banker named Tatsumi with whom he shared a warm friendship during his stay in England. On 30 December Koizumi finished reading the book in the British Museum. His interest in the book is quite understandable when one remembers that one of his main fields was the history of socialist thought. As the entry above shows, Koizumi considered Foxwell to be a better historian of economic thought than Cannan. It is perhaps difficult to agree with Koizumi that Foxwell was a better scholar than Cannan; but it is certainly the case that Foxwell was an accomplished book collector, as his comments to Koizumi demonstrate. Foxwell had first-hand knowledge of bookshops in London and Cambridge. At the time, he had already sold his first collection of about 30,000 volumes to the Goldsmith's Company, and had begun a second collection that he would later sell to Harvard Business School.[3]

In addition to those of Cannan and Foxwell, Koizumi attended lectures by Sidney Webb. A diary entry recounts a lecture of Webb's that he attended on 5 February:

> \Visited Webb's lecture in the evening. This was the last lecture of a series on poor laws. Webb is a very disciplined scholar. His knowledge is wide and thorough. He is one of the best scholars in the world in the sense that he is acquainted with every detail of policy issues. In blunt terms, however, it can be said that he is a scholar with knowledge but without ideas. (Koizumi 1911-14 [2001], p. 332)

Koizumi's last comment on Webb in this passage captures the essence

---

[3] See Ebenstein (2004).

of Webb's scholarship quite well.

In October and November, Koizumi also had an opportunity to attend the lectures of William Cunningham, a Scottish economist with a Hegelian outlook. Koizumi left for Berlin at the end of November 1913 after attending these lectures.

2. *Koizumi as Translator of William Stanley Jevons's* Theory of Political Economy

Shortly before his departure for England, Koizumi completed his translation of William Stanley Jevons's *Theory of Political Economy*, and the translation was published, with a complimentary and subsequently famous introduction by Koizumi's mentor Tokuzo Fukuda, while Koizumi was still in England in 1913. A newly published copy of the translation arrived in London on 16 June. Apparently, a matter had arisen some time earlier concerning the translation about which Koizumi wanted to contact Jevons's son. In his diary entry of 27 January, Koizumi wrote: 'Went to British Museum to study. Investigated the problem of copyright in regard to my translation of Jevons, but am not quite sure. Have decided to a send a letter to his son' (*ibid.*, p. 325). On the next day he wrote: 'Letters and postcards from Shozo Abe; Masahira Takahashi, a skating teacher; and Macmillan. Answer from Macmillan to my enquiry about Jevons's address. The letter said that they were delighted to forward my enquiry to Jevons. But no information on his address' (*ibid.*, p. 325). Shozo Abe, son of the famous founder of Meiji Insurance Company, Taizo Abe, was an intimate friend of Koizumi's, and later became his brother-in- law. This passage shows that Koizumi contacted Macmillan, the publisher of Jevons's *Theory of Political Economy*, to obtain Herbert

Jevons's address, but that the publisher did not furnish it. He succeeded in getting the address in the end, however, and made an appointment to meet with Jevons in June. Before the meeting, Koizumi had to prepare; he wrote: 'Bought a silk hat in the city. For the appointment with Jevons tomorrow' (*ibid.*, p. 383). The following day, after the meeting, he recorded the following:

> This entry is solely concerned with giving a description of Jevons. In brief, he is a country man. He is bald, with whiskers and beard. His hair is partly grey. Dressed in crude, roughly striped clothes with a white Panama hat in hand. His eyebrows are very clearly defined. His eyes are child-like, and when he laughs, he looks like a small boy. Before meeting him, I had been somewhat worried about how to begin our conversation, but after meeting him I felt really relaxed. I had lunch with Jevons. Talked about his father's relationships with Marshall, and also about what had happened if Jevons had not died so young. At first sight, I thought he had something in common with engineers – frugality, steadiness, and unpretentiousness. I soon realised that this first impression was right. He had initially studied natural science, going to Germany to study geology. He also taught geology at the University of Sydney. He tried economics for the first time as a teacher of the subject outside of the university. 'Like the career of my father', he said. After returning from Australia by way of Japan and America, he taught economics at the University of Wales. But he was forced to quit, since he is pretty busy with his work. His current project is to build a garden village in Cardiff. He is an owner of the company. (*Ibid.*, pp. 384-5)

Koizumi's description accords with the facts of Herbert Jevons's life.[4] Son of William Stanley Jevons, one of the three stars of the Marginal

Revolution, Herbert

Stanley Jevons studied geology in Heidelberg. From 1902 to 1904, he taught mineralogy and geology as a lecturer at the University of Sydney. Coming back to Britain, he secured a position as a lecturer at the College of South Wales and Monmouthshire, Cardiff. His teaching experience in Australia brings to mind his father's stay in Sydney almost fifty years earlier.

By the time of his conversation with the young Japanese economist, Jevons had already published *The Sun's Heat and Trade Activity* (1910). Jevons was subsequently to go to India to contribute to the development of economic science in that country, through such activities as participating in the founding of the *Indian Journal of Economics*.

The elder Jevons's relationship with Marshall was a natural subject of interest for Koizumi. It is well known that Marshall's review of *Theory of Political Economy* included frosty comments on Jevons, indicative of the differences in standpoint between the two great economists. Jevons was certain that he had revolutionised economic science. Marshall acknowledged Jevons's contribution, but tried to integrate the new economics into the English Classical School. The ill- fated economist William Stanley Jevons, who drowned at the age of 46, was another topic of Koizumi's conversation with Herbert.

3. In Pursuit of Books

Since online booksellers were not available at the time, scholars needed to hunt down books one at a time, searching from bookshop to bookshop.

---

[4] The following description is based on Tomlinson (2004).

Koizumi was no exception; during his stay in England, he looked for both new and used books at a number of bookshops in London.

On 15 November 1912 he visited the Times Book Club. There he ordered the English translation of Max Stirner's *The Ego and His Own*, a book that stimulated the young Hegelians, including Karl Marx, to explore new directions in their thought. Entries in Koizumi's diary show that the Times Book Club continued to be a source of books for him during his stay in England. However, he had to look elsewhere when it came to older books. The following entry, dated 24 December 1912, records one such foray: 'Bought postcards of suffragettes and K. Marx, *Value, Price and Profit* (3£), at Henderson's at Charing Cross Road' (*ibid.*, p. 308).

Value, Price and Profit is a succinct work that captures the essence of the Marxian way of thinking quite well. The English version mentioned by Koizumi in this entry appeared in 1897; the German version, titled *Lohn, Preis und Profit*, appeared in 1898. Koizumi also bought a work of Kropotkin at Henderson's: 'I forgot to write it down. Coming back from the British Museum yesterday evening, I bought Kropotkin, *Appeal to the Young*, at Henderson's. I read it on the train' (*ibid.*, p. 326). On one visit to Henderson's, Koizumi had an interesting conversation with a German social democrat. The following passage, from his diary entry of 18 March 1913, describes this encounter:

> Many things happened today. After stopping by second-hand bookshops on the Charing Cross Road, I bought Bernstein's *Evolutionary Socialism* at Henderson's. The owner showed me a volume of old German journals [newspapers?], titled *Republik der Arbeiter*, bound together. The year of publication was 1851 and the publisher was Weitling. I never knew that Weitling

> had published such a journal. But I realized that it would have been impossible for him to publish it in Germany; it must have been published instead in New York. To my question 'How much?', he said 'One pound'. I was quite at a loss what to do. I wanted to buy it, but it was quite expensive. Meanwhile, a big man who had just come in took the journal in hand. He seemed to be very interested in the journal, and he said, 'I will forward the information to the party. They will buy it'. (*Ibid.*, p. 340)

Republik der Arbeiter was a weekly journal edited by Wilhelm Christian Weitling. It was published from 1850 to 1855 in New York, as Koizumi rightly inferred. As Koizumi was a frequent visitor, the owner of Henderson's knew that he was deeply interested in the history of socialist thought. The unnamed customer appearing in this passage was Julius Köttgen, a London correspondent for *Vorwärts* and a social democrat. Koizumi met Köttgen as described in the passage, and later recorded the following conversation he had with Köttgen:

> Köttgen: I would like to visit Japan. I don't think the Japanese language is difficult. How is the socialist movement in Japan? I know the name of Mr Katayama.
> Koizumi: I think Mr Sakai is a much better socialist than Katayama. Mr Sakai is a pure materialist reproducing what Marx said. Do you agree with Bernstein or Kautsky?
> Köttgen: Kautsky. I am a pure Marxist. (*Ibid.*, p. 341)

Since Koizumi could speak German, and since he recorded this conversation in Japanese, it is unclear whether he and Köttgen conversed in English or German. Obviously, Köttgen was interested in the Japanese socialist movement. The important figures to whom the conversation refers are Sen Katayama, a Japanese communist who died in Moscow, and Toshihiko Sakai, a socialist whom Koizumi regarded highly. At this point in his career, at any rate, he would not have thought that later in life he would be having heated debates with Japanese Marxists.

III. Germany

1. The University of Berlin and the German Historical School

The German Historical School, led by Gustav Schmoller, was still influential at the time Koizumi arrived in Berlin. Naturally, Koizumi made efforts to attend Schmoller's lectures soon after his arrival. In his diary entry of 25 November 1913, he wrote:

> I am not really familiar with Schmoller's books or theories. It is important to me only that I see Schmoller in the halls of the University of Berlin. I was afraid that Schmoller would die before I arrived in Berlin. I was sitting in the front of the hall when I first saw Schmoller, with grey hair and whiskers and wearing a frock coat. I thought that I was lucky. I was glad to have seen Schmoller. The lecture was about class diversification and class struggle, but of course, I could understand very little. Since he speaks slowly and clearly, I will be able to write down the contents of his lectures if I accustom myself to his speech. (*Ibid.*, p. 432)

Koizumi's main interest was British economic thought; the German Historical School was never his concern. Nevertheless, this passage shows that the young scholar felt it worthwhile to come from abroad to visit the lectures of members of the School shortly before the First World War. Schmoller was a leading figure in the younger generation of the German Historical School. Young researchers from Japan, America and England came to visit his lectures; Koizumi was not exceptional in this regard.

A few days after recording this entry, Koizumi made the following entry regarding his visits to the lectures of important colleagues of Schmoller:

> First, I visited Oppenheimer's History of Socialism. At first glance, one cannot tell whether he is young or old. He looks like an old man with grey hair. But he talks with a clear voice and is spirited. I think he must still be young since he is a *Privatdozent*....I returned home but went to the university once more in the evening to hear Wagner's Capitalism vs. Socialism. His voice was hard to make out. Students stood listening his lecture under the lecture platform. I could understand nothing. Pretty tired. (*Ibid*., p. 437)

Although Franz Oppenheimer was not a full professor at the University of Berlin at the time, he was an active scholar. Later in his stay, Koizumi had an opportunity to visit Oppenheimer privately at his home, and they were also able to meet in Japan during World War II. Adolf Wagner was a close colleague of Schmoller, who had already been appointed to a professorship at the University of Berlin. Together with Schmoller, he contributed to establishing the worldwide reputation of German economics.

Another figure who interested Koizumi was Werner Sombart, a professor at the Commercial University of Berlin. Koizumi first describes

Sombart in an entry dated 9 December 1913:

> Sombart has a florid style of writing, affected and ironic. But my impression of him changed completely when I really saw him. He has a sad air, typically Jewish. He talks without intonation. He has whiskers and sunken eyes. Although he is said to be from a rich family, he wears simple clothes. Wearing a striped shirt, he does not look like the author of *Modern Capitalism*. The lecture was about the discovery of the New World at the beginning of modern history, as well as the colonisation wars between Spain, France, Portugal, and England. That was all I could understand. (*Ibid.*, p. 439)

After earning his degree, Sombart found a position at the University of Breslau, where he taught for sixteen years.[5] In 1906 he was named a full professor at the Commercial University of Berlin, and in 1917 he moved to Berlin University. As the well-known author of *Modern Capitalism*, first published in 1902, Sombart was a favourite scholar of students in Berlin. Yet it bears mention that Sombart was not satisfied with his position at the time of Koizumi's visit, for the newly founded commercial universities were held in relatively low esteem in German academic circles.

Koizumi continued to visit Sombart's lectures. Although Koizumi's command of German was rather limited in comparison with his English at the time of his arrival in Germany, he came to understand the content of the lectures much better later in his stay, perhaps in part because of the private German lessons that he took in Berlin. He recorded his

---

[5] For biographical information on Sombart, see Lenger (1994).

progress in his diary as follows: 'No lectures by Schmoller, but Sombart's lectures have already begun. I am delighted to find that I can understand almost half of the content of his lectures. My German has improved a lot' (*ibid.*, pp. 452-3). Koizumi noted additional progress in his entry of 24 February 1914: 'Sombart finished his lectures for the term. He is going to speak on the later development of capitalism during next term. Now I can understand almost the entire content of his lectures' (*ibid.*, p. 469).

2. *War Has Begun!*

When the Austrian Archduke Franz Ferdinand was assassinated on 28 June 1914, Koizumi was playing tennis with a tennis pro in Berlin. The manager of the tennis court came running up to him with a special issue of the newspaper. As recorded by Koizumi, he cried: 'Doctor, it's terrible! War has begun!' (Shinzo Koizumi, *My CV* [in Japanese. *Watashi no Rirekisho*], Nihon Keizai Shinbunsha, 1966. Reprinted in: Shinzo Koizumi, *Collected Works*, Volume 16, 1967, p. 480). Koizumi wrote that nobody, including himself, took this announcement seriously. In his diary entries from the day of the assassination to the day war was declared, there are no hints of the possibility of war. Since Koizumi followed the German media, including newspapers and journals, this might be interpreted as showing that the atmosphere in Germany was rather optimistic with regard to the consequences of the assassination.

A few days later, in his diary entry of 25 July, Koizumi reported the Austrian ultimatum to Serbia, and wrote:

> Anti-war demonstrations of the Social Democratic Party in twenty places

> altogether inside and outside of Berlin. After Sombart's lecture, I visited one of them. In Unter den Linden there was a big protest. Policemen on horseback make a barrier in the street to hold people back. Conflicts between the nationalists and anti-war people are quite interesting. Social Democrats sang a party song to the melody of *La Marseillaise*. In response, nationalists sang *Heil Dir im Siegerkrans*, *Deutschland Deutschland über Alles* and *Wacht am Rhein*. (*Ibid*., pp. 523-4)

Among the songs of the nationalists, *Deutschland Deutschland über Alles*, with its long interpretive history, may be the best known. Although its original message was a call for the unification of Germany and the dominance of a unified Germany over states, Koizumi's description suggests that it was already being sung as a nationalistic anthem at the time of World War I. As Koizumi observed, the German Social Democrats were against the war at the beginning. However, their position changed in August; as Koizumi wrote in his entry of 1 August:

> The Social Democratic Party changed its position. It caved in to pro-war public opinion. The editorials in *Vorwärts* have a pessimistic tone. It goes without saying that the change in position is due to the fact that Germany has been placed under martial law. But it is still debatable whether or not the party would have continued to maintain its position if martial law had not been declared. (*Ibid*., p. 525)

Socialism, despite its call for the labourers of all nations to unite, has often given way to nationalism, especially during wars; this is one of its problematic aspects. The German Social Democratic Party was not immune to this problem. Koizumi went so far as to say that the party's ideology would sooner or later be dominated by nationalism, regardless of the preparedness of the nation for war. Later, Koizumi came to be known as a sharp critic of Marxism; the change of position on the war of Germany's social democrats may have contributed to his future scepticism concerning Marxism.

Koizumi also criticised the chauvinism of some Germans in Berlin. He wrote:

> They seize and attack foreigners on the street, saying they are spies. Many foreigners have been killed. There is no proof that they are spies. Based on the available facts, it is clear that none of them are spies. After a special issue of the newspaper reported that the British ambassador had requested his passport, mobs attacked the British embassy. They broke windows and threw stones. A Spanish diplomat who came out of the embassy had a terrible experience because he was confused with a Briton. (*Ibid.*, pp. 531-2)

Koizumi later expressed a feeling of comfort with British economic literature as well as the British way of thinking. In a nutshell, Koizumi was an Anglophile, and obviously not a Germanophile. A certain degree of fanaticism associated with chauvinism is unavoidable during a war, but Koizumi's experiences in Germany shortly after the outbreak of the war did not leave him feeling at home in Berlin. In any case, he had to leave Germany soon after with his compatriots. Japan had decided to support England, making it impossible for Japanese nationals to remain in Germany.

IV. Epilogue and Concluding Remarks

Koizumi left for England via the Netherlands with Japanese friends. During his second stay in England, he spent most of his time in Cambridge, where he had opportunities to attend lectures by Arthur Cecil Pigou and John Maynard Keynes. However, neither of them impressed Koizumi. The lectures of Pigou were not quite comprehensible to Koizumi. Keynes was still young, unknown on the international scene of academia. Even after the *General Theory* was introduced to Japan, it does not seem to have influenced Koizumi. In his collected works, one does not find a trace of Keynesian economics. Koizumi belongs to the older generation of economists whom the new economics did not affect. After a fairly short stay in France, Koizumi returned to Japan on 24 March 1916. This concluded his experience of living abroad.

The perspective of the lectures Koizumi attended during his stay was in essence historical, in keeping with the state of economics at the time.[6] Among the lecturers he encountered in England, consider the examples of Cannan and Foxwell. Apart from being a textbook writer at the time, Cannan was more or less an historian of economic thought, as evidenced by his principal work, *A History of the Theories of Production and Distribution,* as well as his role as an editor of *Wealth of Nations.* Foxwell was an accomplished book collector, as his huge collection of economic

---

[6] In this sense it can be said that both Fukuda and Koizumi, his pupil, studied under the strong influences of German economics, especially the German Historical School. Tamotsu Nishizawa said: 'Fukuda once wrote, "When I was a student at the Higher Commercial School in Tokyo, I often prayed that I would be able to attend a lecture by Wilhelm Roscher just one time"' (Nishizawa 2001, p. 156). Compare the above statement of Fukuda with the comment by Koizumi in the diary entry of 25 November 1913.

literature shows. In Germany, Koizumi attended the lectures of Schmoller and Sombart, eminent figures in the German Historical School. Koizumi's personal opinion of Schmoller aside, it was almost a necessity for those studying economics in that period to attend Schmoller's phenomenal lectures. This demonstrates clearly that Schmoller still enjoyed great academic prestige in the period leading up to World War I. All of these lectures pre-dated the formalisation or mathematisation of economic science.

■ REFERENCES

Dahrendorf, Ralf. 1995. *LSE: A History of the London School of Economics and Political Science, 1895-1995*. Oxford: Oxford University Press.

Ebenstein, Alan. 1997. *Edwin Cannan: Liberal Doyen*. Volume 1. London: Routledge/Thoemmes Press.

Ebenstein, Alan. 2004. 'Foxwell, Herbert Somerton (1849-1936)', in Donald Rutherford (ed.), *The Biographical Dictionary of British Economists*, Volume 1, Bristol: Thoemmes Continuum, pp. 403-5.

Koizumi, Shinzo. 1913 [1969]. *Jevons, Keizaigaku Junri* (in Japanese. Translation of William Stanley Jevons's *Theory of Political Economy*), Dobunkan, reprinted in Shinzo Koizumi, *Collected Works*, Volume 24, Bungei Shinju. Koizumi, Shinzo. 1928 [1969]. *Keizaigaku oyobi Kazei no Genri* (in Japanese.

Translation of David Ricardo's *Principles of Political Economy and Taxation*), Iwanami Bunko, reprinted in Shinzo Koizumi, *Collected Works*, Volume 23, Bungei Shinju.

Koizumi, Shinzo. 1933 [1967]. *Marx, Fifty Years After His Death* (in Japanese: *Marx Shigo Goju Nen*), Kaizosha, reprinted in Shinzo Koizumi, *Collected Works*, Volume 7, Bungei Shinju.

Koizumi, Shinzo. 1949 [1967]. *Criticism of Communism: Common Sense* (in Japanese: *Kyousan Shugi Hihan no Jyoushiki*), Shinchosha, reprinted in Shinzo Koizumi, *Collected Works*, Volume 10, Bungei Shinju.

Koizumi, Shinzo. 1966 [1967]. *My CV* (in Japanese: *Watashi no Rirekisho*), Nihon Keizai Shinbunsha, reprinted in Shinzo Koizumi, *Collected Works*, Volume 16, Bungei Shinju.

Koizumi, Shinzo. 1911-14 [2001]. *A Diary of Young Shinzo Koizumi from 1911 to 1914: Tokyo, London, and Berlin* (in Japanese: *Seinen Koizumi Shinzo no Nikki: Tokyo London Berlin*), Keio University Press.

Koot, Gerard. 1987. *English Historical Economics, 1870-1926: The Rise of Economic History and Neomercantilism*. Cambridge: Cambridge University Press.

Lenger, Friedrich. 1994. *Werner Sombart 1863-1941, eine Biographie*. München: C.H. Beck.

Nishizawa, Tamotsu. 2001. 'Lujo Brentano, Alfred Marshall, and Tokuzo Fukuda: The reception and transformation of the German Historical School in Japan', in Yuichi Shionoya (ed.) *The German Historical School: The Historical and Ethical Approach to Economics*. London: Routledge.

Robbins, Lionel. 1997. 'A student's recollections of Edwin Cannan', in *Economic Journal*, June 1935. Reprinted in Alan Ebenstein, *Edwin Cannan: Liberal Doyen*, Volume 1. London: Routledge/Thoemmes Press.

Sugihara, Shiro, and Tanaka, Toshihiro. 1998. *Economic Thought and Modernization in Japan*. Cheltenham: Elgar.

Sugiyama, Chuhei, and Mizuta, Hiroshi. 1988. *Enlightenment and Beyond*. Tokyo: University of Tokyo Press.

Sugiyama, Chuhei. 1994. *Origins of Economic Thought in Modern Japan*. London: Routledge.

Tomlinson, Tom. 2004. 'Jevons, Herbert Stanley (1875-1955)', in

Donald Rutherford (ed.), *The Biographical Dictionary of British Economists*, Volume 1. Bristol: Thoemmes Continuum, pp. 593-5.

CHAPTER 5.

Yukichi Fukuzawa and Confucianism in the Edo Period

Masamichi Komuro(小室正紀)*

I. Introduction

Yukichi Fukuzawa (福澤諭吉, 1835~1901) was able to grasp accurately the basic elements of modern civilization and Japan's situation at the time, and to present a direction for the nation to move forward at the beginning of the Meiji period. This paper considers why such thinkers as Fukuzawa appear on the stage of Japanese history comparatively early. Specifically, it asks why an individual like him came along in Japan before anyone else did in any other Asian nation. Through the episodes of the Opium War (1840-1842), China for instance came into contact with the Western world far earlier than Japan. However, no one in China was able to analyze the trends of the modern ages in

* Emeritus Professor of Keio University

the same way as Fukuzawa did until the Chinese revolution of 1911. In that sense, there is much value in understanding how someone like Ykichi Fukuzawa was able to appear right after the opening of Japan to the West.

The first half of Fukuzawa's life fell within the Edo period (1603-1867). The following is a famous quote from his *An Outline of a Theory of Civilization*:

> "We have lived two lives, as it were; we unite in ourselves two completely different patterns of experience."[2]

This expresses the way Fukuzawa's generation witnessed two different worlds in the Edo and Meiji periods. Fukuzawa was born in 1835 and passed away in 1901 at the age of 66, which means that he was 33 during the Meiji revolution (明治維新).

Fukuzawa also confessed in *An Outline of a Theory of Civilization* that his generation studied mainly traditional Chinese literatures and Confucianism. Fukuzawa himself actually studied only them until he was 19.

II. The Criticism of Confucianism as a Tactics for the Debate

Therefore, there is a need to assess to what extent the education of Confucianism had an effect on the development of the ideology of

---

[2] Yukichi Fukuzawa, *An Outline of a Theory of Civilization*, 1875, (translated by David. A. Dilworth & G. Cameron. Hurst, in *The Thought of Fukuzawa 1.* Tokyo: Keio University Press, 2008) p. 4

Fukuzawa's generation. I believe that the intellectual tradition of the Edo period is a necessary condition for the early appearance of the thinkers such as Yukichi Fukuzawa.

However, Yukich Fukuzawa is very famous as a caustic critic of Confucian tradition. For example, he is known to have said in his autobiography, *Fukuô Jiden* (福翁自伝):

> "It is not only that I hold little regard for the Chinese teaching, but I have ever been endeavoring to drive its degenerate influences from my country."[3]

As evidenced by this quote, many of Fukuzawa's works express a strong criticism of Confucianism and Chinese teaching.

However may we take these anti-Chinese-teaching and anti-Confucianism comments literally? This is the important challenge in understanding Fukuzawa's full intents. Fukuzawa strongly believed that Japanese needed to build and develop a new kind of modern society. For this challenge, he felt that the continuous leaning of the Chinese teaching was a serious problem that needed to be solved, and therefore advocated that people should stay away from traditional Chinese teaching.

Thus, Fukuzawa's criticism of traditional Chinese teachings was due to an opponent or phenomenon that he needed to criticize in order to grab the attention of the public. In this way, Fukuzawa's criticism of Confucianismwas rather meant as a way to spark a debate.

---

[3] Yukichi Fukuzawa, *Fukuô Jiden*, 1899, (translated by Eiichi Kiyooka, *The Autobiography of Fukuzawa Yukichi with Preface to the Collected works of Fukuzawa*, Tokyo: The Hokuseido Press, 1981), p. 216

III. A Certain Appreciation of Confucianism

At the same time, when considering the works of Fukuzawa carefully, one can spot numerous instances in which he did not necessarily criticize the Confucian culture and spirit he held. In some cases, he praised a certain historic role of the Confucianism during the Edo period. There are a few notable instances.

First, in a passage from his autobiography, he assessed the Confucian values and spirit that existed within himself while talking about his father Hyakuske Fukuzawa(福澤百助):

> "From the writings he (Yukichi's father) left, I know that he was a Confucian to the very heart. Among the great scholars on Chinese philosophy, my father had a particular respect for Itô Tôgai (伊藤東涯) and was literally living the old saying "Be true and sincere, unashamed even in the innermost privacy".
>
> My father's ideas survived him in his family."[4] (Additional explanations from the author included in brackets, ( ), throughout the paper)

In the above remark, Fukuzawa was not criticizing the ethical teachings of Tôgai Itô, but rather regarded them as a proud symbol of the traditions of the Fukuawa family learned under Tôgai.

There are further instances of support for the Confucianism. In the autobiography, Fukuzawa records that he has expressed great anger towards somebody else according to his emotions only once. He explains that he has been able to keep away from anger for the following reason:

---

4 *Ibid*, p. 3

> "One day while reading a Chinese book, I came upon these ancient words: "Never show joy or anger in the face." These words brought a thrill of relief as if I had learned a new philosophy of life. Since then I have always remembered these golden words, and have trained myself to receive both applause and disparagement politely, but never to allow myself to be moved by either"[5]

Fukuzawa states that he considers these teachings to represent the direction in which he should live his life. The idea not to express one's feelings of joy, anger, love, and sadness was a pillar of Chu Hsi philosophy (朱子学) or neo-Confucianism, and Fukuzawa indicated that this was something he strongly upheld in his life.

Second, Fukuzawa stated that his general education was based on Confucianism. In the autobiography, he explained that he had attended a private school that taught Chinese classics at the age of 14 or 15, and wrote the following:

> "I changed school two or three times, but I studied (Chinese classics) most under the care of a master named Siraishi (Siraishi Shôzan, 白石照山). Under his guidance I made rapid progress, and in four or five years I had no difficulty in studying a good part of Chinese classics."[6]

Fukuzawa left the home castle town for Nagasaki(長崎) and began to learn Dutch studies at the age of 19. What he meant by the phrase "in four or five years" in the above statement was that he had spent

[5] *Ibid,* p. 19

[6] *Ibid,* pp. 7-8

most of his time learning Chinese classics under Shiraishi. Moreover, he also stated that:

> "While most of the students gave it (Tso-chuan, 春秋左氏傳) up after reading three or four volumes out of the fifteen, I read all—eleven times over—and memorized the most interesting passages. Thus in the course of time I became zenza, or senior disciple who had privilege of giving occasional lectures."[7]

The Tso-chuan is considered to be of a high level of Confucianism. In the above quote, Fukuzawa stated in a modest way that he was ready to be "senior disciple". However, this shows that he had much confidence in the Chinese classics, as he had already read the book times and known by heart the important sentences of it. The above statement shows that he was a parson of fairly rich Confucian knowledge.

Third, Fukuzawa looked back on history and appreciated some developments of the Confucianism in the second half of Edo period. There are such examples in his works, particularly in *The Popular Discourse on National Power* (*Tsûzoku Kokkenron,* 通俗国権論), that was published in 1878. Since the Meiji Revolution in 1868, Japan had been accepting most Western influences as positive. However, in the period around 1878, a certain tendency to believe blindly the Western matters began to be found in Japanese society. In the following excerpt from *The Popular Discourse on National Power*, Fukuzawa warned against the blind belief for Western culture and showed that Japan, during the Edo period, had never been a nation that lacked intellectual progress.

---

[7] *Ibid,* p. 8

> "In the course of Tokugawa's peaceful reign, Japanese scholarship made considerable progress. Scholars studied Chinese classics to be superior to Chinese themselves. In particular, the school of Jinsai Itô (伊藤仁斎) and his son Tôgai (東涯) and the school of Sorai Ogyû (荻生徂徠) threw suspicion on Chu Hsi (朱子) philosophy to advocate a revived study of the classics. We should regard their intellectual insights as matchless, though there are positive and negative opinions about their schools. In the long course of Tokugawa's 250 years, not only Jinsai and Sorai schools but also various Confucians, Buddist monks, writers and doctors could be found throughout Japanese Society. There were few who did not know the titles of *Lun-yü* (*Rongo,* 論語) or *Great Learning* (*Daigaku,* 大学) even in lonely or remote villages, except for extremely ignorant or poor people."[8]

Besides, in the sentences followed this excerpt, he also wrote that the literacy rate among people in the late Edo period surpassed the rates of the Western world. These truths were not only Fukuzawa's, but modern research has proven that the literacy rate in the late Edo period was higher than that of England during the Industrial Revolution.[9] Therefore, Fukuzawa recognized that Confucian education had assisted in the intellectual progress during the Edo period.

He did not limit this to Confucianism only, but also said that there had been a general spread of intellectuality in the Edo period, particularly since the period from Tenmei (天明) to Bunka (文化) era, 1781~1818 :

---

[8] Yukichi Fukuzawa, *Tsûzoku Kokkenron*, 1878, (edited by Osamu Terasaki, *The Works of Yukichi Fukuzawa Vol.7 - Tsûzoku Kokkenron & Tsûzoku Minkenron,* Tokyo: Keio University Press, 2003), pp. 167-168

[9] Ronald Philip Dore, *Education in Tokugawa Japan*, 1965, (translated by Hiromichi Matsui, *Edojidai no Kyôiku*, Tokyo: Iwanamishotenn, 1970), p. 268

> "Even in all that stagnation (of the Edo period) there actually was some progress, and by the end of the Edo period antipathy to lineage had started fermenting."[10]

Namely, Fukuzawa considered that such progress of intellectuality caused gradually an antipathy to lineage which he described as "my father's mortal enemy".[11]

As such, Fukuzawa accepted the traditional Confucian teachings and elements that were a part of him, and did not necessarily see them as detrimental to his learning. Moreover, looking back on the Edo period, he did not regard Confucian teachings as harmful to Japanese society entirely.

IV. Confucianism during the Edo Period

Confucianism was a belief and educational system that was widely used during the Edo period and had a profound effect on the intellectuals of the time. As such, it is important to understand it to analyze the thoughts of the Edo period. However, while "Confucianism" during the Edo period could be grouped under a single umbrella, there existed many different schools, making it a complex subject to explain. As all of the different schools cannot be examined, the three main types of Confucianism are considered here.

The three main types of Confucianism in Japan were, first, Chu Hsi

---

[10] *op. cit. An Outline of a Theory of Civilization,* p. 84

[11] *op. cit. Autobiography,* p.6

philosophy, second, the school originated with Jinsai Itô (伊藤仁斎) and Tôgai Itô (伊藤東涯), and, third, the school originated with Sorai Ogyû (荻生徂徠). All these three schools are referred by Fukuzawa in the above-citation from *Tsûzoku Kokkenron*.

Confucianism is a philosophical learning that centers on an idealistic moral of man and society, "Do (道)", that is "the Way". The easiest method to differentiate between the three types of Confucianism that were studied and followed in Japan at the time is to look at how each school observed the concept of "the Way".

1) Chu Hsi philosophy or neo-Confucianism

Chu Hsi philosophy or neo-Confucianism was a relative new branch of the 2500-year-old Confucianism that was born in the Southern Sung dynasty in the 12th century. It was a kind of Confucianism that was stronger in belief and much more systemized.

Although it can simply be remembered as a stricter and more complex form of Confucianism, its basic belief holds that the universe, the world, humans, and society are all connected and operate together according to one single natural eternal principle of the moral. Currently, mankind is centered on the belief that nature and human morals are separate elements. In Chu Hsi philosophy, these elements are not considered to be separate in nature, and morals and ethics branch out from this belief. As such, morals and ethics are considered to be an absolute natural laws and the crucial part of life. The elite or the ruling class, above all, are expected to live a life that follows these rules, as the role model of the common people. It is believed that going against these morals and ethics is unnatural and detrimental to the ideal form of society and the universe.

The way to live an ethical life is determined by destiny and cannot be altered. There is a Confucian saying that loyalty, filial piety, brotherly affection and love for one's neighbors (忠孝悌信) are keys to life. A life based on this destined Way is believed to be one without greed. Moreover, Chu Hsi philosophy holds that if members of the ruling class live their life according to natural morals and ethics, then those who are ruled will live in the same manner, thus helping to form a naturally peaceful and moral society. The creation of this kind of ideal society is regarded as the ultimate realization of the Way and the main belief of Chu Hsi philosophy.

This belief is vaguely mentioned in *Great Learning* (大学) by Chu Hsi in the phrase, "Once you reform yourself, your household can stand properly. Once your household stands properly, the country can become stable and in turn, the whole world will be peaceful. (身修而句后家齊,家齊而句后国治,国治而句后天下平.)"[12] The term "you reform yourself" means that one must maintain control over one's sprits through with a moral way of life. This in turn allows one's household to be stable. Using an example from the Edo period, a household is considered to be a vassalage of "daimyo ,大名", the Japanese term for feudal lord. Those vassals of lord were considered to be part of the Daimyo's household. The next term used is "stable nation". Thus, stable households create a stable nation. This "nation" designates the lord's domain, " Han, 藩" in Japanese. If the domain is stable, the final stage can be achieved – that is, a "peaceful whole world", that is peaceful

[12] *Great Learning* (*Daigaku*, 大学), (edited by Tetsuji Tsukamoto, *The Four Confucian Classics* (*Shisho*, 四書), Tokyo:Yûhôdôshotenn, 1921), p. 2

whole country. Thus, Chu Hsi philosophy starts with control over oneself and ultimately holds that the good deeds performed by individuals can lead to a moralistic and sound world.

After the 14th century, Chu Hsi philosophy was the most widely-observed thought and learning along with Buddhism in East Asia. It had a strong impact on Japan in the Edo period, and moreover, the Ming, Ch'ing and Yi (Chosun) dynasties regarded it as the orthodoxy. These dynasties appointed their government officials through the examination about the learning including Chu Hsi philosophy. This explains why scholars in these countries placed a stronger emphasis on Chu Hsi philosophy than Japan.

2) A Japanese Confucianism of Jinsai Itô (伊藤仁斎, 1627~1705) and Tôgai Itô (東涯, 1670~1736)

A Japanese Confucianism, *Kogigaku* (古義学) , was introduced by Jinsai Itô and was fully developed by his son Tôgai Itô. It was the main teaching followed by Fukuzawa's father, and was a form of Confucianism that had been created in Japan in reaction to Chu Hsi philosophy.

Confucianism was originally created by Confucius, who lived from the 6th to 5th century B.C.. His words were recorded in *the Analects of Confucius* (*Lun-yü,* 論語), the main text used for the interpretation and observation of Confucianism. This led Jinsai Itô to go back to the basics and to refer to *the Analects*. He found that many of the beliefs held by Chu Hsi philosophy were not necessarily mentioned *in the Analects*. Jinsai argued that there was absolutely no mention of the moral principle equal to the natural low of the universe. He therefore continued to study *the Analects* and to question true elements that Confucius wanted to advocate. He came to the conclusion that men have an innate sense (人情) allowing them to feel what is good or bad. He believed that this nature had been cultivated to fit with society, and that the Way (道) was realized when men followed their own feeling, which was polished in the ordinary social lives. He held this to be a simpler and more authentic interpretation of Confucianism than that of Chu Hsi philosophy.

Furthermore, Jinsai's thought does not focus on the belief that the ruling class must first live in a moral manner in order for others to follow suit. It holds that anyone can live morally and realize the Way as long as they live their daily lives sincerely. In this light, Jinsai's teaching, Kogigaku, is a much more equalitarian belief system. Jinsai Itô expressed it as follows:

> "'The Way (道)' is the path that all people can walk in their daily lives rather than something that has to be learnt from a better person."

Jinsai further stated that,

> "The great road is a path that not only noblemen but also humble people go along. There are from the king and the nobles to peddlers, hostlers, blind people and the injured. Yet there is no person that cannot walk the great road. It is not the Way if only kings and nobles can walk but men and women of humble can not. It is not the Way if only the wise intellectuals can go along but those who are foolish cannot."[13]

---

13 Jinsai Itô, *The Commentary on Analects and Mencius* , (edited by Shigeru Shimiz & Kôjirô Yoshikawa, *Japanese Ideologies 33 ; Jinsai Itô·Tôgai Itô*, Tokyo: Iwanamishoten, 1971), pp. 27~28

Jinsai Itô defined the terms for realizing the Way as follows:

'All people (四民) who perform their everyday works and show respect to their parents and loyalty to those above them, and who do not betray the trust of others are followers of Confucianism.'[14]

Not only the elite but also all people are deemed worthy of fulfilling the Way. This belief allowed Jinsai and Tôgai Itô to infuse more class equality into Confucianism.

3) Sorai Ogyû (荻生徂徠, 1666~1728) and his Research of Ancient Chinese Words, Komonnjigaku (古文辞学)

Sorai Ogyû took Jinsai Itô's Confucianism and built upon it by pondering the thought process of Confucius and what he used as the basic historical documents. Sirai realized that what Confucius explained to be the most important elements of men and society were the deeds of the kings and sages who had lived before Confucius. They were the prominent kings and sages of ancient China, that is, of the ancient Chinese dynasties (唐虞三代) under Yao (堯), Shun (舜), Xia (夏), Yin (殷) and Zhou (周) . Confucius believed that the ancient China was the ideal society and organization for mankind to pursue.

Sorai believed that to attempt to realize the Way, scholars had to look back at Confucius' process of thinkinng. It was also possible to investigate the original texts that Confucius had used in his own research

[14] Jinsai Itô, *The Questions asked by a Child* (童子問), in *the Iwanami Library,* Tokyo: Iwanamishotenn, 1970, p. 205

on ancient China. These texts were called the "*Six Classics* (六経) ". However, one of the texts has been lost and its any copy has not come down to the later ages, so that the term "*Five Classics* (五経) " is also widely used. Sorai considered that it was necessary for the accurate grasp of Confucius' words to make an objective analysis of the five texts. He believed that understanding the five texts would allow him to find out the truth about Confucius' injunctions.

Advocating the importance of documents in Confucianism, Sorai Ogyû sought to assess things objectively and to make sure that the thought process would be as clear as possible. He also started to believe that the only truths he could trust academically were those that were either objectively true or true from experience. Fukuzawa often argued that one should not fall prey to biases or preconceived notions, and Sorai Ogyû put forward the same argument.

V. Confucianism in the Edo Period and Yukichi Fukuzawa's Thinking

Let us ponder the relationship between Confucianism in the Edo Period and Yukichi Fukuzawa's thinking.

1) Chu Hsi philosophy and Fukuzawa

First, we should explore Chu Hsi philosophy, which has a strong message for individuals to control their morals by themselves. In practice, Fukuzawa's thinking had much in common with Chu Hsi philosophy. For example, in his autobiography, '*Fukuô Jiden*', he expressed his view of morals as follows, succeeding an augment in which he tried to co-ordinate all the physical actions of human beings by natural sciences.

> "In spiritual or moral training, I regard the human being as the most sacred and responsible of all orders, unable in reason to do anything base. Therefore, in self-respect, a man cannot change his sense of humanity, his justice, his loyalty or anything belonging to his manhood even when driven by circumstances to do so. In short, my creed is that a man should find his faith in independence and self-respect."[15]

It would not be strange even if a Neo-Confucian had said the second sentence cited above, though the words "his faith in independence" in the last sentence symbolize Fukuzawa's new modern idea.

In November 1896, there was a homecoming event for the alumni of Keio College in a restaurant near the college, Kôyôkan (紅葉館). At this event, Fukuzawa delivered a famous speech in which he declared that students of Keio College must not only acquire knowledge, but also needed to make sure that their goal in college life was to be a source of morality and a mirror of wisdom in Japanese society.[16]

It is considered something like a neo-Confucian belief to practice a strict individual moral code and to be a source of morality.

In 1869, Fukuzawa wrote the following in a letter to his friend, Tôan Matsuyama (松山棟庵):

> "I dare to say that an independence of each parson is the basis of an in-

---

[15] *op. cit. Autobiography,* p. 214

[16] Yukichi Fukuzawa, *The Source of Morality and an Mirror in Wisdom*, 1896, (*The Works of Yukichi Fukuzawa, vol.15*, Tokyo: Iwanamishoten, 1970), pp. 531~534

dependent family, which is then the basis of independent local area, which is further the basis of the independent nation. For the independence of a parson there is no way beyond the enlightenment of his own knowledge."[17]

The words, "the enlightenment of his own knowledge", ties up with Fukuzawa's emphasis on individual learning and scientific spirits. However, the rhetoric and logic of this sentence are very similar to the already mentioned sentence in *Great Learning* by Chu Hsi. That is, "The virtue of a ruler is the basis of virtuous vassals, which is then the basis of virtuous local area, which is further the basis of the virtuous nation."

As mentioned above, there is something in common between Chu Hsi philosophy and Fukuzawa's thinking. Their common thought is that a parson of strong subjectivity is the basis of all matters. But there is, of course, the great difference between these two ways of thinking. In the case of Chu Hsi philosophy, the moral to individual training is the eternally established moral cords. And it is considered that a moralistic ruler should guide ignorant people down the right path. On the contrary, Fukuzawa did not regard morals as unchangeable. He thought that each independent parson should consider by enlightened knowledge what to attain moralistically. He had no idea that men of high standing should guide those below them. Instead, he thought that the assembly of people who can stand alone moralistically will realize a civilized society.

[17] Edited by Keiogijyuku, *The Collection of Letters by Yukichi Fkuzawa, Vol.1*, Tokyo: Iwanamishotenn, 2001, p. 114

2) Jinsai Itô, Togai Itô and Fukuzawa

The second form of Confucianism found in the Edo period was Jinsai and Togai Itô's school. As mentioned above, Jinsai and Togai Itô's ideology and its promotion of equality shared similarities with Fukuzawa's.

In an episode of the *Autobiography*, he discussed about the decoration by government. Fukuzawa had been called upon by the Meiji government to take up a position as a government official, but he declined the offer. Many believed that the decoration had been an attempt to bring a renowned scholar into the Meiji government. A mediator brought up the offer to Fukuzawa again, and he replied in the following manner:

> "What is remarkable about a man carrying out his own work? The cartman pulls his cart; the bean-curd maker produces bean-curd; the student reads his books. Each one follows his obligation. If the government wants to recognize the ordinary work of its subjects, let it begin with my neighbor, the bean-curd maker. Give up any ideas about my work being special."[18]

Anyone who has read some of Jinsai's works would be aware of the remarkable similarity between this insistence of Fukuzawa and Jinsai's thinking, because Jinsai considered that each ordinary man is able to walk along "the Way", the moral way, carrying out his own work.

But what Jinsai and Tôgai pursued was the virtue that made the existing common society operate smoothly and ideally. On the contrary, Fukuzawa thought that human society should make progress toward a

---

[18] *op. cit. Autobiography* , p. 204

new civilization, changing the existing society. On this point we must not forget the great distance between them.

3) Sorai Ogyû and Fukuzawa

Finally, Fukuzawa's thinking should be compared with Sorai's. As already mentioned, Sorai was a Confucian who believed nothing but confirmed everything empirically or positively. It is often mentioned that in such points Sorai and Fukuzawa shared something in common in their thinkings. Also, in Sorai's opinion man should work upon society actively, and it might be necessary to remake society depending on the circumstances. In these respects, many researchers regard Fukuzawa to be like Sorai.

By the way Fukuzawa's teacher in Chinese literature, Shôzan Shiraishi, was a Confucian scholar under the influence of the Sorai School.

In the *Autobiography*, the strand of Confucianism supported by Siriaishi was mentioned as follows ; "Shiraishi Sensei belonged to the school of Kamei (亀井) and in fact, he worshipped that master of sound philosophy………"[19] Here, the 'Kamei' refers to Nanmei Kamei (亀井南冥) and his son, Shôyô Kamei (亀井昭陽), scholars of Sorai school serving Fukuoka domain. The form of Confucianism that Fukuzawa had studied eagerly in his young days had been rooted in Sorai's thinking.

Apart from this matter of academic attachment, expressions and ideas similar to Sorai's are found throughout Fukuzawa's writing. For example, in '*An Outline of The Theory of Civilization*' there is a paragraph arguing

---

[19] *Ibid*, p. 8

that morals are developed according to existing society, and not vice versa.

> " This is why I say theory or morality should be based upon facts, and not vice versa. One must not do violence to the facts by proposing theories or morals based on sheer conjecture."[20]

Just as in this insistence of Fukuzawa, Sorai attached importance to the facts and wrote about a method for considering real conditions and the morals in ancient Chinese society, as follows.

> "*The Six Classics* (六経) are its facts. *Li-ji* (礼記) and *Lun-yü* (論語) are its theories. Theories should be based upon facts and then morals are built up. If man ignores facts and considers only theories, therefore, there is scarcely a man but confuses his ideas."[21]

The explanation that is given is complex in nature; however, simply put, it means the following: *The Six Classics* were the basic materials about the social system and culture of the oldest five dynasties in ancient China from Yao to Zhou. Confucius used these materials to inquire into the reality of the system and culture. The Book of Rotes, *Li-ji,* and *the Analects*, *Lun-yü,* by Confucius represent the meaning of this reality and the spirits of the society. However, without the existence of reality, no meaning or spirit can exist. The acceptance of this truth is how the Way

---

20 *op. cit. An Outline of a Theory of Civilization* p. 67

21 Sorai Ogyû, *A Discourse of the Way* (*Benndô,* 弁道), (edited by Kojirô Yoshikawa, Masao Maruyama, Taichirô Nishida & Tatsuya Tsuji, *Japanese Ideologies 36 Sorai Ogyû*, Tokyo:Iwanamishoten, 1973), p. 12

is realized, and the main point of this phrase is that one must not stray away from the reality. It is important for one to understand reality objectively by materials.

Though these two thinkers have many ideas in common, there is also, of course, a great difference between them. For Sorai, the ideal society is in ancient China before Confucius. But Fukuzawa regarded modern Western civilization as the ideal. In Sorai's opinion, it should be an excellent ruler who makes a proper social system recognizing the circumstances objectively. But Fukuzawa claimed that each ordinary parson grasp the reality objectively and establish one's own independent life. While both scholars believed in objective recognition, they valued different goals.

As mentioned above, it is difficult to characterize Fukuzawa's thought as a descendant of only one Confucian school, whether the Chu Hsi philosophy, Jinsai School or Sorai School. But it could be said that those schools had prepared some components of Fukuzawa's thought.

VI. Intellectual Circumstances since the Late 18th Century

The intellectual circumstances began to change from late 18th century on.

First, there was the development of Dutch learning. While this is an very important fact to consider in the study of Fukuzawa's thinking, this paper does not focus on this in detail. Another element was that Confucianism became more widespread. Since late 18th century, Confucianism became to be studied not only by professional scholars but also by many common intellectuals. The following statistics reflect this: at the end of the Edo period, 215 domains of feudal loads had established their own schools for vassals, while there were more than 260 domains of feudal loads at the same point of time. Out of those 215 schools, 187 were founded in the second half of the Edo period, after 1750. It seems that the increase of the schools of domains correlated to the spread of Confucianism. In second half of the Edo period, many members of warrior class, samurai, started to learn Confucianism, and its study had become normalized among them at the end of the period.

According to the expansion of the circumstances, new problems emerged, and all the doctrines or schools seemed unsuitable for the contemporary reality of Japanese society. Intellectuals came to feel that Chu Hsi philosophy, Jinsai School or Sorai School were insufficient by themselves. That is why the tendency emerged around that time to pick up and combine the useful parts from different Confucian schools, so-called 'Secchûgaku (折衷学)'. But this tendency had not easily matured as a single systematized thought by the end of Edo period. No one could find any clear answers about how to organize the philosophical components from various schools. In the history of Japanese thought, therefore, the days of 'Secchûgaku' in the second half of Edo period were days of trail and error.

For example, Fukuzawa wrote about the mind of intellectuals in the second half of Edo period as follows, to sum up, in *An Outline of a Theory of Civilization.*

> Since about the end of the eighteenth century, learned men did not clearly realize their ambitions or complaints in society. They made only any ambiguous complaints in their literary works that had no reasonable theories.

> Between the lines, their works revealed a dissatisfaction with their contemporary times.[22]

Namely, Fukuzawa thought that the learned men only made complaints without truly grasping their own assertions.

But around the end of the Edo period there were already some components for new thinking. It was the period when Fukuzawa turned from Confucianism to Dutch or English learning and then met with the thinking of the Western civilization, for example, that of Henry T. Buckle, François P. G. Guizot, Francis Wayland, J. S. Mill and so on. When Fukuzawa read the books by those thinkers, he might have felt he had his eyes opened. He came to understand what "learned men didn't realize clearly", that is, that their predecessors had been groping. Fukuzawa could understand Western civilization very clearly, because there was a long period of groping by many learned men in the second half of Edo period. There were some components at hand to understand the new civilization. The task of Fukuzawa might have been how to systematize those components under a reasonable theory. According to the above-mentioned view, it is not strange that a thinker like Fukuzawa appeared quickly just after the Meiji Revolution.

VII. Conclusion: What Distinguished Japan from Ch'ing and Yi dynasties?

Why did a parson such as Fukuzawa not appear in China during the

---

[22] *op. cit. An Outline of a Theory of Civilization* p. 84

Ch'ing dynasty or in Korea during the Yi (Chosun) dynasty just after the Western impact? I think the difference was caused by the intellectual diversity in Japan in the second half of the Edo period. In those days 200 or more feudal domains almost freely adopted various schools of Confucianism, Japanese classics or even Dutch learning as the educational course for their samurais. Furthermore, many private schools offered various subjects or types of educations. That is to say, there was almost no unified or forced educational policy for the whole of Japan. Perhaps this is the true reason why a scholar like Fukuzawa came along more quickly than in other nations. In *An Outline of a Theory of Civilization*, Fukuzawa stated, "since ancient times, progressive steps in civilization were always unorthodox (異端妄說; translated literally, "heterodoxy and rough opinion") at the time they were first proposed."[23] He also stressed, "We know that the spirit of freedom can exist only in an atmosphere of diversity of ideas and contending views (多事争論; translated literally, "discussions in eventful society")."[24] Fukuzawa himself did not believe necessarily that the Edo period should represent the society much of "heterodoxy and rough opinion" or "discussions in eventful society". He strongly argued against the circumstances of the Edo periods. For Fukuzawa, from the perspective of modern society, the Edo period represented a great disappointment. Nevertheless, it was not as if there were no "heterodoxy and rough opinion " and "discussions in eventful society" and such trends were able to bring about a scholar like him, whose opinions differed widely from the norm.

Let us consider a different case. The Ch'ing or the Yi dynasties stud-

---

23 *Ibid*, p. 14

24 *Ibid*, p. 27

ied types of Confucianism other than Chu Hsi philosophy. For example, the Ch'ing dynasty's evidential school of Confucianism (考証学) and the practical Confucianist branch of the Yi dynasty are two noteworthy examples of different types studied at the time. However, in the Edo period of Japan, there was more emphasis on political rule through warrior's authority than on academics. The relationship between politics and Chu Hsi philosophy was closer-knit in the other two nations than in Japan. Anything traditional in those two nations was considered to be based on Chu Hsi philosophy.

Moreover, in those two countries, there was no rigid class structure like in Japan, and officials were chosen through national exams based on Chu Hsi philosophy. On this account, government officials and scholars were more likely to focus on Chu Hsi philosophy and its beliefs. It was harder for those societies to support divergent opinions, as the belief structure itself was so rigid and concrete. Of course, there were scholars of the Chosun dynasty whose opinions differed from Chu Hsi philosophy. However, various schools of thinking did not appeared, like the Jinsai School or Sorai School which prepared the components for the thoughts of the succeeding generation. Or there were no groping years by many learned men, preceding the Western impact. I think, it is these matters that distinguished Japan from these two countries.

This is not meant to demean those nations' responses or to point the finger at the time it took for some changes to be made. Japan's response to the modern ideologies and its resulting problems may have been quick, but it may also have meant that there was no proper face-off between past and modern ideologies. Instead, it can be argued that though the modern ideologies were accepted easily but superficially in Japan Japanese modernization progressed holding old ideologies in the deep of its heart. For instance, Confucianism saw a resurgence in terms of educational policies in the 1880s, and this can be regarded as a result of the modernization that had taken place before. On the other hand, it can be argued that the true form of modernization proposed by Fukuzawa was never fully realized in Japan.

I believe that in the case of the Ch'ing or the Yi dynasties, the traditional ideological beliefs were so strictly observed that a fundamental battle between the old and the new ideologies was unavoidable, which required a lapse of time that could not warrant a swift response. There were two forms of ideological modernization experienced by East Asia, that is, on the one hand a form to react to the changes quickly and easily and on the other hand a form to need long time for fundamental paradigm shift. Whether a swift response was better is debatable even to this day. Perhaps now is the time for different schools of thought to truly share their experiences and to learn from their mistakes together.

CHAPTER 6.

Kant on China and Confucius*

Eun-Jeung Lee**

I. "Königsberg Chineseness"

It is often claimed that Kant shared certain ideas with Chinese philosophers. In the opinion of observers in both Europe and East Asia, a close relationship exists between Kant and Confucius, particularly in moral philosophy.[1] Friedrich Nietzsche even

* This paper was published in *Damron 201* (『담론201』), Volume 10, No. 1, 2007.
** Leiterin der Koreastudien, Freie Universitaet, Berlin, Germany

[1] Major representatives of modern Neo-Confucianism (including Zhang Junmai, Tang Junyi, Mou Zongsan, Xu Fuguan) argued in their Declaration about the Reevaluation of Sinology and the Reconstruction of Chinese Culture (published 1957), for example, that the Neo-Confucianism of the Song-Ming era was very similar to Kant's idealism. Western idealists had not recognized it because they had been misled by the one-sided explanations provided by the Jesuits, who rejected not only Taoism and Buddhism but Neo-Confucianism as well(Chan, 1957: 545).

dubbed Kantianism "Königsberg Chineseness," most likely because he discerned a certain parallelism between the two.[2]

But Kant's published works make apparent that he did not unreservedly share in the enthusiasm for China prevalent in his day (Lee, 2003: 156-180). In his *Observations Concerning the Sense of the Beautiful and the Sublime* (1764), Kant wrote: "What silly grimaces accompany the many-layered and refined compliments of the Chinese; even their paintings are grimace-like and show wondrous and unnatural forms, of a kind found nowhere else on earth. They also have venerable grimaces, as they derive from ancient usage, and no people in the world has more than they." In a commentary on this 'ancient usage,' he added: "In Peking they still have a ceremony during a solar or lunar eclipse during which, with much noise, they attempt to drive away the dragon who is devouring these heavenly bodies. They maintain this deplorable custom from olden times, even though one knows better" (Kant, 1764: 252). But a passing remark in his *Conjectural Beginning of Human History* (1786) makes it impossible to ignore that Kant, too, was among those who saw in China only a culture gone rigid since antiquity, and hence a backward culture.

Noteworthy here, however, is Kant's peculiar interpretation of the reason for the inflexibility of Chinese culture. In the conclusion to this

---

2 Nietzsche used this term in connection with his critique of Kant as a moral philosopher. In his work *The Anti-Chris*, Nietzsche wrote: "A virtue must be our own invention, our most personal self-defense and relief: in every other sense, it is only a danger. That which is not of necessity to our lives harms it. Virtue pursued only out of sense of respect for the term, in the manner Kant wished it, is harmful. 'Virtue,' or 'duty,' or the 'good in and of itself,' or the good with the character of impersonality and universality –all fantasies of the decline and last enfeeblement of life that Königsbg Chineseness expresses" (Nietzsche 1967: 492).

1786 essay, he states that: "Thus, at the cultural stage at which humankind still finds itself, war is an indispensable means for progress"(Kant, 1786: 121).[3] For "a war that is always feared (forces) even the heads of states [...] to confront and respect humanity," and only in this manner would culture and freedom "be encountered." As evidence for this thesis, "one must only look to China, whose position was likely threatened only once by an unexpected attack, but it has no powerful enemy to fear, and thus in it, every evidence of freedom has been erased"(Kant, 1786: 121). This thesis of Kant's, that war was the precondition for cultural progress and ultimately for perpetual peace, does not need to be analyzed here.

It may be worthwhile, however, to pursue his assertion that "every evidence of freedom has been erased" in China, and to compare it with other statements Kant made about freedom. Thus, in his essay *What is Enlightenment?* (1784), he praised Frederick II, the Great, as enlightened particularly for granting religious freedom, calling his reign an Era of Enlightenment (Kant, 1784: 40). One then must ask oneself why he ignored the policy of religious tolerance the Chinese Emperor Kangxi[4] pursued, though he was aware of it, as one can see from the transcript of his *Course of Lectures in Physical Geography* of 1770. This is particularly puzzling because what needed to be tolerated in Germany were merely variants of Christian belief, while it China it was a matter of fundamentally different religions, including Buddhism, Taoism, and Christianity. Kant

---

[3] Kant continued: "and only in a culture that is (God knows when) mature would a perpetual peace be beneficial for us, and only through it then be possible." Is "continuous war" for Kant then the precondition for achieving "perpetual peace?"

[4] Chinese Emperor Kangxi (1662-1722) promulgated the so-called Tolerance Edict in 1692, which legally placed Christianity on the same footing as Taoism and Buddhism, thereby assuring Christians throughout the country freedom to promulgate the Gospels. On this, see Collani, 1989: 11.

thus used two different yardsticks, which one cannot justify or explain away by merely claiming his insufficient knowledge of China.

II. Kant's Lectures on Physical Geography

By contrast with Kant's published works, the numerous manuscripts of his lectures on physical geography show not merely comprehensive knowledge of China on his part, but also the incoherent manner with which he dealt with the information available to him at the time (Lee, 2003: 174-180) – though this was also true of many other scholars in his day. At the same time, these many sources permit one to follow the way in which his image of China changed over time.

From 1756 and 1796, Kant gave the *Course of Lectures on Physical Geography* at least 48 times, from notes he himself had written. The dictated text that served as a basis for his lectures was crafted already before 1760, and though it was soon outdated, Kant improved on the text itself only to a very limited degree thereafter (Adickes, 1911: 10). Instead, he often modified it in oral presentation (Adickes, 1911: 65). Kant never revised this original text into publishable form, and near the end of the preface to *his Anthropology from a Pragmatic Point of View* (1798), he wrote that in light of his age it would hardly be possible any more for him to transform the lecture text of his *Physical Geography* into a handbook, and "no one other than himself would be able to decipher it" (Kant, 1798: 122). As a result, his *Physical Geography* is known largely in the form of copies of his original, dictated, lecture text and from notes taken by those who attended his lectures.

These texts were all created at different times. The version found in Vol. 9 of Kant's works published by the Prussian Academy of Sciences in the early 20th century, for example, comes from Thomas Rink, a friend of Kant's. It was first published in 1802 under the title *Immanuel Kant's Physical Geography*, and according to Rink, was the text of Kant's lecture series, "issued at the request of the author (Kant) from his handwritten manuscript, in part revised and corrected by him"(Glasenapp, 1954: 3). But Erich Adickes, in his comprehensive 1911 study of the subject, was able to establish not only that Rink's edition was full of holes, but also that it contained many stylistic changes and even additional (and unattributed) commentary by Rink himself. For example, there is commentary about the "newest reports of the English since Macartney's *embassy*." Yet as Kant last gave this lecture course in 1796, at which point only a single report (by Anderson) was available – two further reports, those of Staunton and Hüttner, appeared only in 1797 – this commentary could not have come from Kant himself.

In Adickes's view, as well as that of recent Kant scholarship, the handwritten manuscript given to the Duke of Holstein-Beck, and checked through by Kant, is a more authentic copy of his lecture text (of 1757/58) than that found in the Rink edition (Adickes, 1911: 31). In addition, we have a variety of notes taken by lecture auditors,[5] though some we know of did not survive the war. In what follows, the manuscripts of Holstein-Beck, Herder (1764), Hesse (1770), Kähler (1774), Geo-Pillau (1784), Dohna (1792) and Rink (1802) are drawn upon.[6] In addition, we can utilize Glasenapp's work, as he had manuscripts available to him

[5] These manuscripts are currently being transcribed at the University of Marburg, and will appear in Vol. 26 of the 'Akademie' edition.

[6] These were made available to the author through the kind offices of Dr. Werner Stark at the University of Marburg.

that have not survived.

As these various manuscripts came into being at different times, one can follow the changes in Kant's description and evaluation of China, though one should not compare this with Kant's published works either in form or content. Even the initial, dictated text that formed the basis of the manuscripts noted above was comprised largely of loosely organized, successive notes about different lands and peoples. No even partially exhaustive or comprehensive overviews are contained therein, nor were specific or basic ideas developed. In evaluating Kant's image of China, one should thus always bear in mind that Kant never published his notes himself.[7] At the same time, one should also remember that the "summary view of the most important natural curiosities of all countries, in geographic order" that includes his views on China, were only a kind of appendix to the actual text, only constituting about the last one-fifth of it.

Kant's "Lecture Course on Physical Geography" was primarily concerned with water, atmosphere and the earth, and with minerals, plants and animals; problems of ethnography and cultural history could only be addressed in passing. That is to say, China, Confucius and East Asia only occupy an insignificant part of Kant's *Physical Geography*.

Kant's knowledge of China and Confucius came from the works of other authors, but despite this, he provides only occasional and incomplete references to them. Glasenapp suggests that Kant primarily used translations, such as the 1732 German version of Thomas Salmon's

7 Adickes is even of the opinion that it was only senility on Kant's part that brought him to agree to Rink's edition. "Had Kant remembered the manner in which, many years ago, he had compiled large parts of his text based on a small number of authors, he surely would have denied (Rink) permission to publish"(Adickes, 1991: 286).

Modern History, or the present state of all Nations, and compendia such as the 21-volume *Allgemeine Historie der Reisen oder Sammlung aller Reisebeschreibungen* [the first seven volumes of which were translated from John Green's compilation "A new general collection of voyages" (London), while most of the other volumes were translations of Prevost d'Exiles's "Histoire generale des voyages"] (Leipzig 1747-1774), the *Bibliothek der neuesten Reisebeschreibungen* [Library of the Newest Descriptions of Travels] (Frankfurt and Leipzig 1780), or the 39-volume *Magazin von merkwürdigen Reisebeschreibungen* [Magazine of Remarkable Travel Descriptions] (Berlin 1790-1839) (Glasenapp, 1954: 9f.). To these one might add, as some of Kant's knowledge of China, German editions of works by explorers and researchers held in high repute in those days, including Pierre Sonnerat,[8] Jean-Baptiste du Halde,[9] Engelbert Kämpfer,[10] Peter Simon Pallas,[11] and others. Kant also knew

---

8 As a commissioned royal administrator, he had traveled in Asia from 1774 and 1781. In his report *Voyage aux Indes orientales et à la Chine Fait par l'ordre du Roi, depuis 1774 jusqu'en 178* [Voyage to East India and China, undertaken at the King's orders, from 1774 to 1781], which appeared in German translation (Zürich 1783, 2 vols.), one can read sweeping and highly critical judgments about China. Though he had only visited ports in Canton, and thus could only base his opinion on the statements by Chinese traders and dockworkers, there is hardly a section of this report that has anything positive to say about China and the Chinese.

9 Jean-Baptiste du Halde began publishing letters from the Jesuit missionaries in China in 1708, in Paris, under the title *Lettres édifiantes et curieuses écrites des missions étrangères par quelques missionnaires de la Compagnie de Jésu* [Edifying and Curious Letters, written in foreign missions by missionaries of the Society of Jesus]. In addition, from these sources and other information, he also compiled his 4-volume *Description Géographique, Historique, Chronologique, Politique De l'Empire De La Chine Et de la Tartare Chinois* [Geographical Description, History, Chronology and Politics of China and of Tatar China] that appeared in Paris in 1735.

10 As ship's doctor, Kämpfer (1651-1716) accompanied the Dutch envoys between 1690 and 1692 in their precisely predetermined path through the islands of Kyushu

the works of de Guignes[12] and de Pauw,[13] as well as the reports from the Jesuit missions in China.

In addition, Admiral Anson's 1748 description of his travels apparently served as an important source. Kant's description of the Chinese national character as being that of swindlers is largely identical with the account in Anson.[14] Peter Osbeck's *Reise nach Ostindien und China* [Travel to East India and China] was probably also among the sources he consulted.

---

and Honshu on their way to Edo (Tokyo) to present the Japanese shogun their gifts. Upon his return, he wrote *Das Japan unserer Zei* [Japan in our Times], though it only appeared after his death, in 1727, and then in English translation.

11 Pallas (1741-1811) wrote works about his research and explorations of eastern and southeastern Russia and Siberia, including *Sammlung historischer Nachrichten über die mongoschen Völkerschafte* [Collection of Historical Reports about the Mongolian Peoples] (1776-1802).

12 M. de Guignes, Mémoire dans lequel on Prouve; que les Chinois sont une Colonie Egyptienne [A Report in which it is Proven that the Chinese are an Egyptian Colony], Paris 1760; M. de Guignes, Le Chou-King un des Livres Sacrés des Chinois, Qui renferme les Fdements le leur ancienne Histoire, les Principes de leur Gouvernement & de leur Morale; ouvrage recueilli par Confucius [The Chou-King, one of the Sacred Books of the Chinese, which contains the fundament of their ancient history, the principles of their government and their moral code; a work taken down by Confucius], Paris 1770.

13 C. d. Pauw, Recherches philosophiques sur les Egytiens et les Chinois [Philosophical Research on the Egyptians and the Chinese (Berlin 1773).

14 In Holstein-Beck and Rink's manuscripts one can read that the Chinese poisoned living pigs, threw them overboard, and then fished them out again. This is likely an abridged version of the account given Anson's travel report (see R. Walter, A Voyage round the World in the Years MDCCXL, I, II, II, IV. By Georg Anson, London 1748. Reprinted London 1974, pp. 355-6). In it, one can also read about the practice of stitching the urinary bladder of pigs closed; Herder had noted this as well from Kant's lecture. See J.G. Hder, Nachlass der Staatsbibliothek Preußischer Kulturbesitz in Berlin, HN XXV 44, B1. 5v.

Adickes was able to establish that Kant did not just read and evaluate his sources: he often used passages from them, verbatim.[15] This is likely also the explanation for why Kant's statements frequently contradict one another, as in his comments about the Egyptian origin of Chinese culture.[16] Thus, in 1770, Kant claimed that of all countries on the earth, China was the oldest. Even Egypt can not have been inhabited that long, because due to the flooding of the Nile, one has to believe that the sea once covered all of lower Egypt, and that the Nile built it up slowly with its mud. China, by contrast, is an elevated country. According to the oldest information that we have, China was as thriving and appointed as it is now. In proportion to its expanse, it is the most complete country in the entire world (Kant, MSb: 185).

By contrast, in 1775 and 1772, respectively, he opined that "The Chinese appear to be the descendants of the Egyptians,"(Kant, 1775, Ms Berlin 1296: 309, quoted in Glasenapp, 1954: 99) and that "Desguignes believes that (the Chinese script) developed from that of the Chaldeans"

---

15 That Kant not only relied on the content of his sources but also often copied them word for word should not unduly surprise, given the attitudes about intellectual property in his day; see Adickes, 1991: 285. In addition, this was for his own use and for that of his auditors.

16 The thesis of the Egyptian origin of Chinese culture had been proposed long before by Athanasius Kircher in *China [...] illustrat* [China … Illustrated] (1667) that claimed the Chinese were the descendents of Ham, who had moved with his people eastwards out of Egypt toward Persia, and later toward Bactria. Colonies from Bactria had, after all, reached China. De Guignes renewed this argument in the 1760s and 1770s, though de Pauw objected – correctly, though for the wrong reasons, inasmuch as he noted the incalculable gap between the advanced civilization on the Nile and the lack of culture among the Chinese would have made such contact impossible. See C. de Pauw, Vol. I, p. VIII. As it was, de Pauw had nothing good to say about China, as he, among other things, wanted to undermine the widespread Sinophilism that existed in certain circles at the time. See Lee, 2003: 176.

(Kant, 1772, Ms Berlin 398: 465, quoted in Glasenapp, 1954: 99). In Herder's notes, one finds something similar: "M. de Guignes believes Chinese is debased Phoenician" (Herder, HNa). Why Kant chose one or another interpretation cannot be determined from the available material.

It is also not possible to establish why Kant occasionally modified his judgment of Chinese culture. His list of the basic characteristics of this culture remained largely unchanged over time: the Great Wall, the porcelain gate in Nanking, the many canals, the large population, the deceitful tendency of the Chinese, their laws and science, and so forth. Yet certain differences emerge from the manuscripts in how they are depicted, an example of which can be seen in the treatment of religion in China. Thus, in the Holstein-Beck, Herder, and Rink manuscripts, Buddhism (or "the sect of the Fo," as it is called) is noted as the religion with the largest number of believers, or is called the national religion. In Hesse's manuscript, by contrast, one reads: "They have maintained the religion from olden times, as absurd as it is. They do it so that the man in the street will not perceive that the Mandarins can make mistakes. They are also not very ardent in their religion. They have two kinds of priests, the bonzes and the lamas. The first come from the old Chinese, the latter from the Tartar religion"(Kant, MSb: 193, see Ft 27).

In Kähler's (1774) manuscript one reads by contrast: "Their religion consists of the five King (Jing) or holy books, those of Confucius." (Kant, MSc: 482) But according to Geo-Pillou's notes (1784), "their national religion is very mixed. Much in it has been declared to be religion by the bonzes, much declared to be religion by Confucius. The 5 Kings are holy books of the Chinese" (Kant, MSd: 358-359).

Which selection criteria led to such differing depictions will probably never be clarified, but one thing one can glean from the manuscript dates is that what began as a generally positive assessment increasingly turned negative. One cannot find in the later manuscripts anything like his description of China as "the most civilized [country] in the entire world, or "elevated," as one can in the Holstein-Beck and Hesse manuscripts. And while the mention of inferior mathematics and antiquated astronomy is in the Holstein-Beck and Herder manuscripts relatively neutral, by the time of the Hesse manuscript Kant has become more critical: "they have no geniuses, and their science does not advance to higher levels"(Kant, MSb: 187). Indeed, in the Geo-Pillau manuscript (of 1784), one reads: "As far as the sciences in China are concerned, each (scholar) tries to surpass the next one. It is not a nation that has a higher opinion of its own sciences, but also not one that works at it with more endurance than the Chinese. ...... They have not a single science, though they have arts, and they can not even prove the few theorems of geometry that they know, but are instead merely practical. Much has been made of their astronomy, but they have no theory; instead, their science is only based on tables"(Kant, MSd: 352-353).

Kant spoke in a similarly dismissive vein in a 1785 manuscript that Glasenapp examined: "Do we want to ask whether they have other sciences? The answer is: not a one, for they even count wood to be one of their elements"(Kant, Ms 2596: 182, cited in Glasenapp, 1954: 97). This disdainful judgment was continued in his later reflections on physical geography. In a note dated 1789, Kant wrote: "(Remarkable that to the Chinese the world is square). The limited nature of the Chinese is shown: 1. in their paintings that have no shadows, either in portraits or on buildings; 2. in their script, which calls for a good 80,000 characters to make oneself understood rather than our 24; 3. in that they do not travel to other countries; 4. that their religion (of the Fo) has its head outside of China"(Kant, 1802: 621).[17]

Kant also changes his kind about the significance that should be accorded to Confucius. Though he had no problem calling him "the Chinese Socrates" in the Holstein-Beck manuscript, in the Hesse manuscript he was of the opinion that "rather than philosophy, the Chinese have a kind of moral code," namely teachings "that everyone knows already, even without them." Furthermore, whereas Kant, according to Herder's excerpt (correctly) dated him as living 500 years before Christ, the Hesse manuscript says that Confucius lived about 300 years before Christ's birth. "(Kant, MSb: 191) According to the Kähler manuscript, the five "Kings" (Jings) "or holy books" of the Chinese, "come from Confucius," but contain nothing but dry ethical doctrine (Kant, MSc: 482). And according to the Geo-Pillau manuscript, Kant claimed: "Their erudition contains many things that although they are learned are not really proper science. Confucius is their greatest philosopher, of whom they say, that he possessed all wisdom, and alone he had once asked what the highest good was." In this version, Confucius is a man "who lived in Socrates' time" (Kant, MSd: 354, 358).

Finally, in the (now no longer extant) text that Glasenapp examined, Kant's scorn is even clearer: "Philosophy is not to be found in the entire Orient, a few wise Arabs excepted. Their teacher Confucius does nothing in his writings other than to provide moral lessons for the rulers ......

[17] Who would have expected such a full-bodied judgment from this great philosopher? asks Glasenapp. He contradicts Kant's arguments, point for point: Didn't Kant know that the spiritual head of the non-Italian Catholics around the globe lived outside of their home country? And what of Kant himself, who had never been outside of the immediate environment of his native city? Had Kant forgotten that China was a country the size of Europe? Glasenapp, 1954: 98f).

and provides exemplars of earlier Chinese rulers ...... but an idea of virtue and morality has yet to occur to the Chinese."(MS 2599: 305, cited in Glasenapp, 1954: 103f.)

Apparently following Sonnerat (1783: Vol.2, 12f.), Kant also doubts the accounts of the Jesuits: "These peoples were much praised some time ago, so that in retrospect, one could believe that in many ways that no better land existed than this China. But the missionaries sent by Rome had too many prejudices and reasons for doing so, as they wanted to prove something to the world. Since then, the language has noticeably changed. They want to still praise parts of it, but because the truth is far too plain to see, this will redound (on them)" (Kant, MS 2596: 197, cited in Glasenapp, 1954: 97).

It is thus not surprising to find Kant, as in the Geo-Pillau manuscript, raising doubts about the good-naturedness and virtue of Chinese rulers, so highly praised by the Jesuits. In fact he tries to prove the opposite: "As far as the behavior of the Emperor is concerned, this is much praised, and he himself writes about affability, but we merely want to examine his deeds. In 1748 and 49 he wiped out the Tatars, ... He also sent them to Siphan, and they were a people who had lived independently for many centuries. The Emperor sought them out in order to conquer them, at which he succeeded, upon which he destroyed the entire kingly house, other than one single girl, whom he kept for show"(Kant, MSd: 357).

Kant did not doubt in the least that the Chinese ruler was a despot with the power to decide over the life and death of his subjects. By law, these subjects were in any case obligated to be obedient and deferential toward the authorities, and the same was true of behavior toward parents. These were the highest laws of the Chinese, to which courtesy and compliments would have to be added. Kant mentions these laws in every manuscript, though he presents the well-known Chinese moral codes relatively dispassionately and without adding his own interpretation.

He did sometimes explicitly mention these laws, however, and did not mince words. The law on the obedience of children to their parents, Herder noted in 1764, was "political and was intended to strengthen obedience toward the emperor"(Herder, HNa). In the Hess manuscript, it states: "this subservience of the children toward their parents leads them to slavish behavior toward the authorities"(Kant, MSb: 192). The most remarkable comments, found in a form unique to this manuscript, are recorded Geo-Pillau: "As far as the laws of the Chinese go, they serve only to keep the people quiet and subservient to the emperor, but in the process, no attention is paid to morality. ...... Children must obey [their parents], but not for reasons of morality, as the parents have absolute power over them : they can throw them away, kill them, or otherwise do with them what they will. ...... Parents are given this power by the authorities so that they can gradually accustom their children to despotic rule, but also to make marriage easier, as the Emperor wants to see his states populated"(Kant, MSd: 356).

Kant's claim that Chinese laws were not about morality, even if made only mentioned in passing, deserves particular attention as it reflects Kant's critique. By putting it this way, Kant states that the Chinese are without moral autonomy and reason.

One can only conjecture why Kant, in denying the Chinese moral autonomy, assigned them to those peoples whose basic principle was to be found only in the eudemonic (that is, whose highest ethical goal is happiness and personal wellbeing) but not in the elutheronomic (that is, those who follow the principle of freedom through the internal setting of laws) (Kant, 1785: 393-405; Kant, 1797: 378). In his view, earthly happiness is "the complex of all possible human ends attainable through nature whether in man or external to him"(Kant, 1790: § 83, 431), due not to the autonomous acts of humans but instead to the "charity" of nature. The "material" which makes up the means to influence happiness include power, wealth, honor, health, affluence and contentment with one's own situation (Kant, 1785: 393; Kant, 1797: 480-481). Together they form the "complete satisfaction" of all "wants and inclinations"(Kant, 1785: 393). In that sense, Kant was of the opinion that the principle of one's own happiness would call for as much insight and discernment as possible, but no other reasons would determine the will than would be appropriate to the capacity for low desires (Kant, 1797: 384-388). And since the reports of the Jesuits again and attain stressed the well-ordered nature of life and high moral standards in China, Kant may have concluded that the Chinese were primarily concerned with "sustained well-being" and a "pleasurable life," or in other words with happiness.

That would have been a remarkable transformation, since only a few decades before, philosophers like Leibniz and Wolff had held the morality of the Chinese in high esteem precisely because they saw in it evidence of an ability of humans to reason that was independent of divine revelation. As Kant was quite familiar with their enthusiasm for Chinese philosophy, one can ask why he did not try to justify his opinion to the contrary. In addition, as Kant knew the translated Confucian classics as well as the writings of the Jesuits, he could well have mentioned that Confucian philosophy was much more than the moral code of the Chinese. Leibniz dealt with this in quite a different manner.[18] But one

[18] For example, in his *Lettre sur la Philosophie Chinois* [Letter on Chinese Philosophy],

searches in vain for comparable indications in Kant, and his bold assertions are that much more astonishing given his scant knowledge of Confucian teachings. His assertions do not go beyond the widespread, disparaging contemporary opinion of the 5 *Jings* (Kings), for example (Kant, MSd: 359). Though Kant knew that the Chinese laws rested on these five books, it appears he made no attempt to directly examine the books containing the teachings of Confucius in order to come to his own judgment. He could have read these books, because they existed in Latin translations, which were widely read in Europe at that time. The book "Confucius Sinarum Philosophus sive scientia Sinensis latine exposita," which was published by Philippe Couplet and other Jesuit missionaries 1687 in Paris, contained a biography of Confucius and the translations of *Lunyu, Daxue and Zhongyong*. In 1711 "Sinensis imperii libri classici sex" written by François Noël was published in Praha; it included first translation of *Menzius' Xiaojing and Xiaoxue* (Lee, 2003: 38-54).

In that sense, one can ask whether Kant's distaste for the Confucian moral code should be understood as a rejection of Confucian philosophy. Glasenapp, at least, makes an effort to give Kant's critique of a Confucianism deeper philosophical meaning: "First, Kant misses the keenness of expression, the logical connections, the rigor of proof, and the systematic and comprehensively organized arguments in the philosophical works of the Chinese. ...... The Chinese philosopher is not trying to convey insights based on rational conclusions; instead, he wants to solve the mysteries of life intuitively and renders what he perceives in the form of aphorisms. Those accustomed to thinking in Western ways

---

Leibniz considers the term *li* and *qi*, the leading ideas of the neo-Confucian Xingli School (Leibniz, 1968).

will thus see Confucian sayings as disconnected sentences without philosophical foundation"(Glasenapp, 1954: 132f).

But Glasenapp's explanatory effort is problematic inasmuch as it provides no clues about how Kant could perceive such deep philosophical differences without having made an effort to address Confucian or rather Chinese philosophy. In this synopsis of Chinese philosophy, Glasenapp also shows himself to be attached to the common clichés that existed in the West at the end of the 18th century.

III. Conclusion

In fact, in Kant's shifting evaluation of Chinese culture, one has a reflection of the changing stages in interpretation and evaluation of China of his contemporaries. In light of the fact that he was wholly dependent on the literature about China and had no first-hand knowledge of the country, it may appear understandable that his views were shaped by the opinions of the day. On the other hand, one also has to ask what reason Kant had to set his own misgivings aside about the unreliability of the reports written by traveling merchants. He was quite aware that the unfavorable reports of the Chinese came from commercial centers on the Chinese coast, and says himself (in the 1772 manuscript), "the people there are all rogues"(quoted in Glasenapp, 1954: 97).

By contrast, his judgment of China in the first years of his lecture course on *Physical Geography* were influenced by the positive, or at least neutral, tone of the Jesuit reports, even if already at that point he remarked on the deceitful character of the Chinese (a impression that he had adopted from Anson's report of his travels). Given the lack of importance of China in Kant's thinking, one might want to disregard his contradictory and inconsistent attitude towards the country and its culture, but that does not justify his sweeping, at best one-sided, and in any case not sufficiently substantiated, judgments.

■ REFERENCES

Adickes, Erich. 1911. *Untersuchungen zu Kants physischer Geographie.* Tübingen.

Chan, Carsun. 1957. *The Development of Neo-Confucian Thought* Vol. 2. New Haven.

Collani, Claudia von. 1989. *Eine wissenschaftliche Akademie für China. Briefe des Chinamissionars Joachim Bouvet S.J. an Gottfried Wilhelm Leibniz und Jean-Paul Bignon über die Erforschung der chinesischen Kultur, Sprache und Geschichte.* Stuttgart.

Glasenapp, Helmuth von. 1954. *Kant und die Religionen des Ostens.* Kitzingen-Main.

Herder, Johann Gottfried. (HNa). *Herdernachlaß der Staatsbibliothek Preußischer Kulturbesitz in Berlin,* HN XXV 44, B1. 5v.

Kant, Immanuel. 1764. "Beobachtungen über das Gefühl des Schönen und Erhabenen." in: Wilhelm Weischedel(Hrsg). 1983. *Kantwerke in zehn Bänden*– Sonderausg. Darmstadt. Bd. 2, SS. 823-884.

Kant, Immanuel. 1764a. "Untersuchung über die Deutlichkeit der Grundsätze der natürlichen Theologie und Moral." in: Wilhelm Weischedel(Hrsg). 1983. *Kantwerke in zehn Bänden* – Sonderausg. Darmstadt. Bd. 2, SS. 739-773.

Kant, Immanuel. 1775. "Von den verschiedenen Rassen der Menschen zur Ankündigung der Vorlesungen der physischen Geographie im Sommerhalbenjahre 1775." in: Wilhelm Weischedel(Hrsg). 1983.

Kantwerke in zehn Bänden – Sonderausg. Darmstadt. Bd. 9, SS. 9-30.

Kant, Immanuel. 1784. "Beantwortung der Frage: Was ist Aufklärung" in: Wilhelm Weischedel(Hrsg). 1983. *Kantwerke in zehn Bänden* – Sonderausg. Darmstadt. Bd. 9, SS. 51-82.

Kant, Immanuel.1785. "Grundlegung zur Metaphysik der Sitten" in: Wilhelm Weischedel(Hrsg). 1983. *Kantwerke in zehn Bänden* – Sonderausg. Darmstadt. Bd. 6, SS. 7-102.

Kant, Immanuel. 1786. "Mutmasslicher Anfang der Menschengeschichte." in: Wilhelm Weischedel(Hrsg). 1983. *Kantwerke in zehn Bänden* – Sonderausg. Darmstadt. Bd. 9, SS. 83-102.

Kant, Immanuel. 1790. "Kritik der Urteilskraft>" in: Wilhelm Weischedel(Hrsg). 1983. *Kantwerke in zehn Bänden* – Sonderausg. Darmstadt. Bd. 8, SS. 235-650.

Kant, Immanuel. 1797. "Die Metaphysik der Sitten" in: Wilhelm Weischedel(Hrsg). 1983. *Kantwerke in zehn Bänden* – Sonderausg. Darmstadt. Bd. 7, SS. 303-643.

Kant, Immanuel. 1798. "Anthropologie in pragmatischer Hinsicht." in: Preußischen Akademie der Wissenschaften(Hrsg.). 1907. *Kant's gesammelte Schriften Bd.* VII. Berlin.

Kant, Immanuel. 1802. "Physische Geographie." in: Königliche Preußischen Akademie der Wissenschaften(Hrsg.). 1925. *Kant's gesammelte Schriften Bd.* XIV. Berlin, Leipzig.

Kant, Immanuel. 1964. *Aus den Vorlesungen der Jahre bis 1762 bis 1764. Aufgrund der Nachschriften Johann Gottfried Herders* (Hrsg. v. H.D. Irmscher). Kantstudien Ergänzungshefte 88. Köln.

Kant, Immanuel. (MSa). Manuskript von Nachschrift der Vorlesung "Physischer Geographie". Ein dem Herzog v. Holstein-Beck überreichtes, von Kant durchkorrigiertes Heft (Holstein-Beck).

Kant, Immanuel. (MSb). Manuskript von Nachschrift der Vorlesung "Physischer Geographie" von 1770 (Hesse).

Kant, Immanuel. (MSc). Manuskript von Nachschrift der Vorlesung "Physischer Geographie" von 1774 (Kähler).

Kant, Immanuel. (MSd). Manuskript von Nachschrift der Vorlesung "Physischer Geographie" von 1784 (Geo-Pillau).

Kant, Immanuel. (MSe). Manuskript von Nachschrift der Vorlesung "Physischer Geographie" von 1792 (Dohna).

Lee, Eun-Jeung. 2003. "Anti-Europa." in: *Die Geschichte der Rezeption des Konfuzianismus und der konfuzianischen Gesellschaft in Europa seit der frühen Aufklärung*. Muenster, London.

Leibniz, G.W. 1968. *Zwei Briefe über das binäre Zahlensystem und die chinesische Philosophie* (Übers. v. Renate Loosen / Franz Vonessen). Stuttgart.

Nietzsche, Friedrich. 1967. "Der Antichrist." in: *Friedrich Nietzsche Werke in zwei Bänden*. München. Bd. II SS. 482-545.

Sonnerat, Pierre. 1783. *Reise nach Ostindien und China in den Jahren 1774-1781*. 2 Bde. Zürich.